dub

FINDING CEREMONY

alexis pauline gumbs

Duke University Press *Durham and London* 2020

© 2020 Duke University Press
All rights reserved
Printed in the United States of America
on acid-free paper ∞
Designed by Aimee C. Harrison
Typeset in Neuzeit S, Sabon, and Arnold Boecklin
by Copperline Book Services.

Library of Congress Cataloging-in-Publication Data
Names: Gumbs, Alexis Pauline, [date] author.
Title: Dub : finding ceremony / Alexis Pauline Gumbs.
Description: Durham : Duke University Press, 2020.
Includes bibliographical references.
Identifiers: LCCN 2019032704 (print)
LCCN 2019032705 (ebook)
ISBN 9781478005414 (hardcover)
ISBN 9781478006459 (paperback)
ISBN 9781478007081 (ebook)
Subjects: LCGFT: Poetry.
Classification: LCC PS3607. U5459 D83 2020 (print)
LCC PS3607.U5459 (ebook) | DDC 811/.6—dc23
LC record available at https://lccn.loc.gov/2019032704
LC ebook record available at https://lccn.loc.gov/2019032705

Cover art: Canleen Smith, *Space Station Monk-Ranger*, 2014. Photograph by Cecil McDonald Jr.

for all
(my relations)

contents

ix   a note

request   1
commitment   3
instructions   5
opening   7
whale chorus   15
remembering   21
nunánuk   34
Boda   40
Anguilla   47
another set of instructions   66
red august   74
relation   92
prophet   94
and   110
skin   114

120   losing it all
126   it's your father
145   edict
153   edgegrove
163   unlearning herself
177   birth chorus
194   conditions
199   Jamaica
202   blood chorus
214   shop
220   orchard
227   cycle
231   saving the planet
239   staying
246   letting go

acknowledgments   253
notes   261
crate dig   273

*After and with published uncollected essays
and one interview with Sylvia Wynter.*

a note

So I have to be realistic and say how can I expect people whose *discipline is their identity* to accept this hybrid model? When what they/we are being faced with is the total removal of their discipline as an autonomous field of inquiry? But then think of the dazzling creativity of the alternative challenge that would be opened up?

—Sylvia Wynter, speaking to Katherine McKittrick in "Unparalleled Catastrophe for Our Species? Or, to Give Humanness a Different Future: Conversations," in *Sylvia Wynter: On Being Human as Praxis* (emphasis in the original)

Sylvia Wynter learned every colonial language. She studied the philosophical and theological patterns in the understanding of life, personhood, and environment leading up to colonialism based on a core proposition: if the ways of thinking, being, and understanding that made colonialism and slavery imaginable were constructed over time, and heretical to the ways of thinking, being, and understanding that came before them, it must be possible to understand life, being, and place differently by now.

Throughout her prolific career, Wynter has used theory, fiction, drama, and continual critical conversations to get at the underside of the stories so core to our existence that we don't even track them as stories. As a participant in multiple social movements, and as a key part of the transformation of the humanities and social sciences in the US academy (while also critiquing the scope of both the political movements and the academic tendencies of her time), Wynter has argued that scholars in the humanities, and cultural workers more generally, have a responsibility for what is and is not imaginable in their lifetimes. Police brutality, the destruction of the physical environment, the theft of resources from the so-called developing world, and every other horror of our time are based on a dominant and now-totalizing understanding of what life is, a poetics of the possible.

I wrote this book based on moments of emphasis in essays and one interview with Wynter over several decades. Each source text was written at a different time, spoken in a different place and for different people. And though the emphasis is different based on the audience, and though the way *in* may be different depending on where she is standing, she tells us over and over again how we got *here*. The inhumane history of man. The violent imposition of a supposedly universal humanism on variably dispossessed communities. And she implores us, at this moment, when, because of the planetary scale of communication, she believes there is actually a chance for a real universalism or a real species-level interaction with the universe, to tell a different story. As she says over and over again, *all of our lives depend on it.*

> It never came linearly. It tends to come the way a flower blooms. It comes unexpectedly; and it has nothing to do with "genius." It has to do with this beginning to question your own "consciousness." It's the idea of *poesis*, again; there is also *a poesis of thought*; *a new poesis of being human.* These concepts don't come in a linear fashion. They build up. They build up, you know? So as you're talking they build up and they build up the way music builds up and up and up until you get that sudden. . . .
>
> —Sylvia Wynter in an interview with *Proud Flesh* magazine

It can be dangerous to investigate what our lives depend on, to recognize that freedom requires a species-scale betrayal of our founding mythologies. I should have known that sitting with Wynter's demand for heretical poetic action against our deepest beliefs every morning would prompt me to unlearn myself. And though I wanted intimacy with her ideas, I didn't realize how close to home this unlearning would be. If *Spill* took me to the contemporary afterlives of slavery and *M Archive* took me to the postdated evidence of our imminent apocalypse, *Dub* eviscerated me of my own origin stories, the fragmentary resources I had used to make sense of my own life.

In my sci-fi short story "Evidence" and on the last page of *M Archive: After the End of the World*, there is a woman in a cave writing a record with her menstrual blood, as a message that will live beyond her time. In her recent writing and conversations, Sylvia Wynter talks about a cave too, found in South Africa and called "Blombos Cave." It dates back 100,000 years, and the ochre writing on the wall is not blood, it's paint, made to look like blood, one hundred millennia ago. Sylvia Wynter's challenge to the species is this: what if what we think is blood, is just paint? What if what we believe is required of humans by nature is just a story that we told ourselves about what being human is and what nature is? What if who we think we are, what we believe at a gut level about our kinship loyalty and our perceived survival needs are responses to a story we made up and told ourselves was written by our genes? And what if one group of people colonized the whole world with a story that survival meant destroying life on earth? What then? And by then, Sylvia Wynter means now. She does not identify as a science fiction writer. Instead she argues what the humanities have been relating to as the history of the human has all been insidious science fiction, a fiction about what science is, written deep in our neurological responses, science fiction at best, horror fantasy at worst.

Wynter says we are not *Homo sapiens*, we are *Homo narrans*, not the ones who know, but the ones who tell ourselves that we know. She says we therefore have the capacity to know differently. We are word made flesh. But we make words. So we can make ourselves anew. Inspired by Wynter, I conducted an experiment on the scale of one life connected to all other lives, on the scale of three hundred individual mornings connected to every dawn of existence. I made myself a dare. What if I go to my own veins, the origin stories that I think precede me, what if I go there and say that all the blood that ever spilled can now become paint. What then? And by then I mean now.

As I started doing the daily writing that would become this book, I started to hear from the perspective of my ancestors from the Caribbean region. And then my Irish ancestors who shipwrecked into the Caribbean and stayed. And then beyond the Caribbean region. My coastal whale-listening Shinnecock ancestors. My untraceable Arawak ancestors. My Ashanti ancestors who survived the Middle Passage. And then the ocean itself. In each case, I found myself confronting stories that I had been told, or that had been told around me, or that had been silently providing the context for my racial, national, and cultural existence. But these stories emerged in different voices, from submerged perspectives. And as I opened to a new and threatening listening (that often left me sitting at my computer in shock), my sense of who were and were not my ancestors shifted.

Relatives outside what we understand to be the human species had some storytelling and untelling to do as well. And as I sought to understand the species of whales, coral, barnacles, bacteria, and so forth, that were speaking from the bottom and the surface of the ocean, I began to understand that the scientific taxonomy of what constituted a species or which family, phyla, genus, in some cases even kingdom and domain, a particular form of life was, was as debatable and discursively unstable as the narratives within my family of who was an inside or an outside child, and who was related and why and how, and certainly as complex as what Wynter teaches us about: the discursive construction of man.

I had to understand that when I reached out for my ancestors I couldn't (like population geneticists do) just stop at some point of relation that would be marketably salient to my ego's prior understanding of who I am now. My listening began to include speakers who have never been considered human. And while that category of the never-considered-human tragically includes my enslaved ancestors, my disabled ancestors, my queer and indigenous ancestors, and everyone subject to the police radio codes Wynter writes about in *No Humans Involved*, it also generatively includes whales, corals, barnacles, bacteria, and more. Kindred beyond taxonomy.

This writing, and Wynter's rigor, required me to let go of my voice and to surrender to language practices outside my memory and education. It required study into the political content and context of places I have never lived and during times that I have not been alive. It required repetition and giving over to the timing and rhythm of prayer, it has required me to read each page aloud at least a dozen times and to know that I am not the same person and the room is not the same place when these words have been spoken. It has required me to trust and know myself intimately and in the same moment to stop knowing who I am.

PROUD FLESH: "So we can make the connection between what you call poesis, the breaking down of the status-quo order of 'Man' and something like dub poetry, for example."

SYLVIA WYNTER: "Exactly! The whole world is organized about this aesthetics of rhythm, you know?"

Dub is a poetic work made from the doubling journey of a queer Caribbean diasporic Black feminist writer. I am sampling the emphasis and breaks of Wynter, a world historical Caribbean theorist who is about my grandmother's age. Influenced by the promiscuity and prolificity of dub music, the confrontational homegrown intimacy of dub poetry, and the descendants thereof (especially D'bi Young Anitafrika's sorplusi method, which I write about elsewhere), this work depends on and disrupts rhythm and riddim, the impact of repetition and the incantatory power of the spoken broken word.

This project is an artifact and tool for breath retraining and interspecies ancestral listening. It is structured to ask, what if you could breathe like whales who sing underwater and recycle air to sing again before coming up for air? What if you could breathe like coral from a multitude of simultaneous openings connected to one source built upon the bones of all your dead? What if you could breathe like cyanobacteria who made the sky into oxygen millions of years ago and sent their contemporaries to a world of sulfur deep under ocean and ground? What then? And by then I mean now. These are the ceremonies I found. You will find, especially if you read aloud, but even if you don't, that many of these passages ask of you what my ancestors are asking of me. When you think it's time to come up for air, go deeper. When you think your heart will break, stay there, stay with it. But at the same time, when you think you gotta hold onto something (like who you think you are), let go.

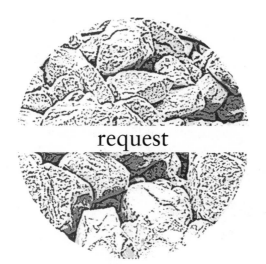

request

we would like it if you wrote us poems. we would like it if you wrote us long life sentences. we would like it if you broke sentences and gave us more life than you or we were told could be contained. we would like it if you remained. we would like it if you showed up every day. we would like it if you drank water. we would love it if you would turn off your phone. we would sincerely appreciate it if you stopped pretending to be alone.[1]

commitment

we promise to wake you up if we think you won't get the point of the dream. we promise to show up if you show up. every day. we promise to make you feel sick when you lie to yourself. we promise to let love through if it's love you came to do. we promise to make time flexible if you give us all your time. we promise to think of you more often than you think of us. we promise to remember you when you forget. we promise to be wherever and in everything you haven't noticed yet. we promise to be we, even one by one. we promise to outsmart your mind. we promise to overlove your heart. we promise to echo over your voice. we promise you everything. everything. all we ask.[1]

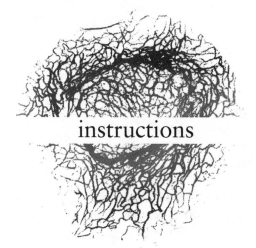

instructions

tell them about the eastern shore and running. tell them about underneath the boat. the hard shell breaking open. the land so wet it's water. the water so hard we live on it most the day. tell them how we left and how we stayed.

tell them about the whales. but tell them using the oyster shells. tell them about wampum and waiting. tell them about the salted dirt within you. tell them how we found each other again.

tell them about the shells. tell them about the giant turtle shells. tell them about the soup we made in shells when we needed armor. tell them why we needed armor and what we did before the harm. tell them about flint, magic, coral, god, and fire. and what we left to tell the tale.

tell them about the whales. and how they swam next to us singing. how they breathed sometimes bigger than the boats. what they taught us about evolution. how they clicked sometimes louder than the chains. how they taught us to make time out of salt. how they deepened our lungs. opened the top of our heads. how they made their whole bodies into drums to show us how it would be.

tell them who taught you to dream. to stay. to breathe. and then show them who taught you to leave.[1]

opening

if you gathered them they would be everyone.

gather them.

recognize in them your jawline, your wet eyes, your long-fingered hands, seeking what but this multitude. if you gathered them they would not fit on this island. they would spill back into the ocean whence they came. when you gather them they will have fins and claws and names you do not know.

gather them anyway.

some will look you in the eye, some are too microscopic to see. if you don't gather them all you will never be free. if you gathered them you could not hold them, scold them, demand back what you think is lost. gather them today or your soul is the cost. gather the ones who sold and who bought and who tossed overboard. gather the erstwhile children in the name of the lord. gather the unclaimed fathers, the ones with guns and with swords. gather them up. with your hands. with your relationship to land. with your chin set. you are not done yet. you never will.

gather them more. gather them still.

they will unfound you and surround you unfind you and unwind you travel to you unravel through your own needle. gather the thread. collect your dead.[1]

put yourself in the center and draw them in. stand where you standing which is not under and not over. you. not gonna get over it. and where you stand is not always standing either, is it? sometimes quicksand sometimes bended knee, very often that cross-legged thing you do, sitting on the floor or hugging your own legs like they were people. be where you are and draw them to you. you might need to move your hands, one of those legs or a book from blocking your heart. that would be a good start. put your arms out like if you were floating in water. daughter. they know where to find you.[2]

this is what we did. we put everything where it needed to go. we knew about need by intuition. we knew about need by experience. we knew about need by not needing what we thought we needed. we needed you to know something else. so this is what we did. we knotted up our knowing with our needing. we kneaded back our needing into notthisnotthennotagain and we knew the net of our needing, the need of our knowing would wander and would wait. we knew it like we knew salt. we knew it like we knew bait. we know it like we know you. don't hesitate.[3]

first, the sound. you hear it even if no one else does. even if you wake and already don't remember. second, the seconds. you feel the up-tick in your heart bringing you back into time. third, the rise. as if you are pulled vertical across the floor and before you know it you have taken several steps. it is a minute or so before you are you as you know you. in the rising you could be any of us.[4]

save the top of your head for the water. don't let the nonsense burn it out. cleanse with salt and coolness. thousands of years ago it was a spout. place your head in places worthy. place your hands over your heart. bless yourself with generations. that's a start.[5]

what the coral said:

breathe. breathe. breathe. sing. let that water move within you. let it
be you. let your every cilia dance you into healing. let the warm salt
water brighten you. your tears. sleep. and when you dream of work-
ing, sleep again. sleep until you dream of floating. dream until your
edges soft. dream until you birth yourself in water singing with the
bones of all your lost. dream until you breathe not from your mouth,
not from your nose but through your hair and through your skin.
dream until you claim the ocean. breathe until you feel no need to
swim. breathe until your dreams flow out your brain. breathe and let
them in your heart. breathe and we will call you again. that's a start.[6]

there are very few things that you must do. this is one. this will show you the others. there is a difference between assignment and need.[7]

whale chorus

it's not the world on our shoulders, it's the ocean on our hearts. on top of our whole torsos, actually. we get round beneath it. the weight that tries to lift us, the pressure that spreads like if love was sonic and could get everywhere, the sound of your unasked-for heartbeat, like if you were the center of something, stretching to try to make the globe not break, like without you the world would crack and lose itself. it's more like that.

they say god moved over the face of the deep, but in the deep there we already were. already pulsing, already pulled by moon, relevant to us whether or not it was lit by sun. they fear the depth of the ocean rightly. we know what it means to be encumbered under there. we know what it is to have no choice but to pull from the bottom of ourselves daily. we don't have the luxury of surface. whether or not we want it.

ever wonder why an island woman loves a clean floor? looks down without missing anything? sweeps even the dirt in the yard? well, where do you think we live while you sleep? down here. at the bottom of everything.[1]

who do you think thought of the ocean? we who would be whales. how could we prepare for the lives we evolved into. immersed in a substance we could not breathe. and nevertheless called to be graceful. huge in ways that the world could not hold. except by these means. unbound by the limits of time. because we thought of the ocean before we became who we are. how could we know the selves we had never been. how could we know places we had not the bodies to see. how do we breathe across generations. ask yourself. this is not the power of positive thinking. this is no birthday wish in smoke. this is existence or absence. no joke.[2]

between you and me, we knew it would never work. just because the singing of the whales had caused bumper stickers and rallies and international bans on their murder and the criminalization of the exploding harpoon (you know. that thing that got under their skin and destroyed them from the inside) didn't mean it would work for us. i mean how long had we, black women, been singing.

when they decided the whale was an intelligent creature, nuanced, descriptive, they decided that the people who killed them were greedy, were savage, were less evolved. isn't that interesting. the same people who forced the whaling indigenous into sale instead of ceremony now spoke of evolution. spoke of the humane and didn't choke. this is why we didn't have much hope. our intelligence and the multiple forms of proof required did not inspire the world to disentangle its hooks from our looks and our attitude.

we assert that it was not the song of the whales that saved them. if singing could save we'd be god. it was the fact of other sources of oil to move onto, other deep black resources to extract. it was a fact. they could only save the whales once they knew they didn't need them. it was as simple as that. and they haven't found a way yet to say it. their needles in our skin, targeting us where we breathe. which is everyone we love. trapping us below and yet detracting us above. chasing us across oceans. they risk their very souls. they know it though. they need us more than gold.[3]

so we listened. and we started with the top of the head. we listened from the opening of the womb for the futures not yet forgotten. borne not of brain but higher. and at the moment of birth sometimes lower. but we listened. in warm rooms of waiting shaped like the stomachs of whales.

if we were whales why would we eat ourselves. why would we turn our bodies into heat and light for the whole community. ask it again. if we were not whales what would we do. waste ourselves. nourish nothing. leave our people cold. and what for?

if we were whales then we would know about choosing. about re-membering. about remembering an even older self that knew land. about coming back to the belly of the people, to the circle of the story. when you remember, put yourself there. in the belly of the whale. let yourself return. learn what it takes to come from water and find legs and then leave your legs to find water and to hear with your mouth and find lungs and wings in everyone around you.

there is an older story. if you want to know. about a big enough love for winter. a love deep enough to come back.[4]

i would sing you the shape of the world between us. turn my body into drum to let you know. slam my skin onto the surface of the ocean to tell you. i am here. wherever you are.

if it's dream you listening for. i'll dream you. if it's poetry in the morning. whatever. the radio. just test me. there is nowhere i cannot be. there is no sound i cannot travel through. there is no you i don't surround.

you can look or not look. you can fill your days with running in the shoes of other people. you can suffocate the minutes. i have time. i do not leave you. you can muffle every moment with your fear. it doesn't matter. i'm still here. and i am here. and i am here.[5]

remembering

you. basically our dreams were you. our nightmares too. can you imagine what it looked like from here? of course you don't have to, do you. the space, the colors, at the same time the dullness. we dreamt and we thought it was us, but it was always you. and you dream and you think that it's you, but it's always us. remember that.

sometimes in our dreams you were a bird. or that was us . . . the calling birds and owls reminding you. sometimes you were a wall covered with words. sometimes you were all the other people you know. sometimes we are all the other people you know. usually our dreams were of school. where we didn't get to go. where we went and got abused. where they told the lies about us. where you always are, we've noticed.

sometimes in your dreams you paint us with pieces of books you have read that we didn't write. somewhere you read that we didn't really write. but we did. and we do. i mean look. not just here in the book. look. your face.[1]

some of us were here because we were stuck. some of us were here because we were stuck on believing other people needed us in order to get unstuck. some of us were here for the water, just the look of it, not the need for it. some of us were here for the pleasure, heightened by the pain of suffering, activated by the unavoidable repetition. some of us were here for others of us. just to see them again in form. just to form them again in seeing them. some of us were here for no reason. it was completely unreasonable for us to be here. some of us were here for our own names. to reclaim them. some of us were here to repay something that couldn't be repaid. some of us were here to get laid, and get the rest of us here. some of us couldn't be bothered. some of us were here to be mothered or fathered better than what happened or more. some of us were not really here, but just seemed to be. we were the ones guarding the door. you came here because we called you. you called you. the you that was us. before.[2]

there was a time when we thought no one would ever understand. even that, as we say it, presupposes time. as you understand it. and that's not what we mean. what we mean is how could you. how could you understand imperatives outside of time. how could you live this daily way if you did. how could the waves we sent become words you could hold, or could they? if they would be flutters in your heart would you yet know them? pulses in your thighs, would you still know what to do? and then you started dancing. all of you. any of you. and that's when we knew to keep sending the messages. that's when we knew that you knew.[3]

we would never leave you. we would never leave you here. we would never leave the world like this. that's why we put you here. you hear us? we put maps behind your eyes and over the entire sky. we put stories everywhere you stepped. but child services would have called it neglect.[4]

the first thing to remember is the smell. no, that's just the last thing that remains. but use it anyway to bring you back to earth, to make your memories solid. to make you long for sweetness. before that comes water and the way you taste it. the way you call it up within yourself. remember. remember. and before that there was heat. the way you changed into you. you the way you feared what you knew. the way you knew when to move and how to stay. and before that day there was the sound that you found. that had followed you around from the stars with just one thing to say:

feel it. you'll be okay.[5]

what do you think? maybe sometimes the breakthrough pulls on your brain. makes the contractions of your heart hard like Pitocin. and you sleep at the bottom of the ocean during the storm. and you feel the moon pull you through all the layers of water. and you let the heat drag you through all the layers of rock. and when you crash against anything you crash against yourself. remember what the ocean told you. there is nothing that is not me. and whatever confuses that, will break selves against themselves against me and still be mine. i am cause and effect. i am me pushing me into meaning. know that and breathe. know that and breathe again.[6]

you had to have a last name. last is a function. and a descriptor. but the types of names that last are the paternal names. and if you give yours away to take on the name of another man or if you keep the one your mother gave hers away for, or if, like with my people, you steal the name in some grab towards impossible accountability it is still never the name of the mother.

which is just another evident example of what you already know. they don't want you to remember me, they don't want you to remember free. they do not want you to know my name. but you know it. don't you?

so then build your memory early in the morning out of secrets and intuition. make your archive out of unauthorized claims. craft your knowing out of water and heat. wake up and write down my name.[7]

when they made me they tapped on the sound between the stars until it rang clear enough to call them back to what they came to do. the sound dispersed across centuries, the rhythm speeding and slowing with the urgency of particular times and particular tides and the particular curves of particular orbits. what you see is just a particle. what can be held by sound, what can seem solid in all this movement, a shimmering stillness so you can know. but the important thing is not to look. it is to listen and find the rhythm. is it speeding up or slowing now. tap tap. tap tap.[8]

do they do that to you too? mistake you for themselves. take you as anyone they love. it's the love does it. wherever you go in the world people try to claim you. something in them is saying they know love when they see it. when they see you first they have already seen you before. everyone's cousin at least. at best. keep it. cultivate love and share it. look at yourself in the mirror, look yourself in the eye like you never saw yourself before. look through time into your own eyes and find me. [9]

there was a thick brown we used. to remember all of it. muck and how we got here. mud and how they stole it. land and what it didn't mean. trees and what they remembered and how they cracked and what they were used for. trees and how they witnessed and whipped and wept. there was the brown of sugar and vanilla and everything they would use to make whiteness. everything they would use to make whiteness, even their own bodies, their own children, also brown. all so brown. dirt. the color of dirt. everything. you did. everywhere. you're going.[10]

you remember the pulse. that broke into stars. you remember the songs and their echoes still floating. you remember the floating before needing breath. you remember that life. that life without death. you remember the crashing. the spacemaking heat. you remember the falling. the blazing bright streaks. you remember explosions and oozing and cooling. you remember the hardening time. you remember the widening. remember the wet. you remember the ocean that breathing begets. you remember the depth and don't ever forget the pulse and the float. you remember the breathing before the boat. you remember the hardening coral notes. you remember the reaching, the clawing, the hands. the need for the sand. you remember the crawling, the suction, the sludge. you remember the slither unleashed from above. you remember the shiver the need and the love. you remember creation. you remember the length and the holding and roots. you remember the dreams and the brightness, the truths. you remember the entrance the closeness the route to the place we now glow. you remember the way and the want and the loss. you remember the distance, the pull and the cost. you remember remembering and jolt and toss. don't forget what you know.

just remember to grow.[11]

go back. it was the kitchen table. it was close enough to a window that you could see yourself in glass. there was something you were looking for but you wouldn't let yourself look long enough. there was something you wanted to ask.

back when? it was the kitchen table. it was the desk. it was the changing table and all the rest. it was the reason we were stable and able and blessed, because we ate from there. and it was not shells. it was only spells made by repetition. prayer made by pounding dough. critique culled by cutting herbs and vegetables down to size. it was not a place where you would gaze into your own eyes, but if you looked you could see your hands.

no one understands what makes the surface steady, what makes the sacred items charged and ready is not what they are. you could make an altar today by what you have scattered around the car if you really trusted. it is not all that. just sit down.[12]

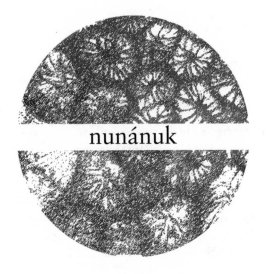

nunánuk

what i didn't do? disappear. float out. forget. prove them right. drop the purpose of my fighting stance. leave my skin and story for buzzards. i did not. do you hear me? what i did was generations. was the nation. maiden to matron. what i did was keep my word to the shore.

what i went through? it was more than the land and the store and the practices and the blood and the mud. we didn't know what it would be called eventually, after the fall. we didn't know how permanent it would be, like you, how could we.

what i knew? i knew wampum and press. i knew how more became less. i knew the gait and the dress. i knew more than them. i knew words i wouldn't say and wouldn't teach and wouldn't name. i knew from the moment they came we would have to keep knowing out our mouths. i knew touch and i knew truth. i knew age and i knew youth. i knew tenderness and proof. i didn't show it though. i knew bit lips to wait. i knew you wouldn't be too late. i knew the half was not our fate. i knew the game.

what i did? i made and i made and i made. i spoke and didn't speak. i learned and didn't let on. i walked and did not faint. i stood and stood and stood. i fed and took away. i placed and faced it all.

my name? is platform and plate. is situation and state. is only rightly spoke by the third generation and the folk. my name is purer than the tanning stoke. my name is calloused hand in stroke. they don't remember it.[1]

if i had to describe her hair, i would say it was economic. specific black waves, protective without nonsense. i would say that. the specific black love she allowed to shape her future. the black indigenous survival she would be, with her people. us. the chosen words and eyes that seemed not to blink, but to shutter, saving everything.

if i had to describe her prayer, i would say economic too. more than that, strategic. less than that, pragmatic. i would say she was asking for a future with dreams tempered by what waves had brought in. to a god that the people-waves-had-brought-in had different names for. tight ideas about. i would say she had come to bargain, but that would be crass. and unfair.

if i had to describe her there on Sunday morning i would say echo i would say mnemonic. i would try so hard all week to remember. i would say let go song quick. i would say let go, without expecting her to let go. i would say let go and be the god i know. but i know she would not say that.

if i had to describe her where, i would say she was in the place that light left through dust. the place after trusting earth. the same place offered her by birth. but stole.

if i had to describe her glare?

control.[2]

maybe she had to say all the names of her people before she said her own name. maybe she had to bend over to clean oyster shells, shine wampum for the scribes. i don't know. her back seems straighter than mine. maybe she sang a lot when she was a little girl at the shoreline.

i want to know how she listened. how she traveled forward and back. how she felt with centuries of known land underfoot. and if she lived inside the bones of whales. i want to know about her breathing before the black dress and the straight buttons. and the church. what did it mean and what was under. lungs. love. leaving.[3]

for mary emily landin

land. you trust it but the water can take it any time it wants. the wind can snatch you up off it at her whim. so you make myths to lull yourself and the children. about how water made you and wind loves you. maybe. maybe, mary. but that don't mean you safe. like your cousin harriet, you used song. vibrational tech, but that's not what you would have called it. you did what your mother did and her mother did when they could. you sang and made them sing to program *home*. you didn't all the way trust the whims of wind and white people. the wooden promises of men. but this is where you had to raise them, so you sang.

you wouldn't have said it like this but you knew. the songs you sang your children, the songs you made your children sing were about being mud and more than mud, water and more than weeping, blue but beyond blue, and connected to a celestial strain, a home bigger than all our pain. a place that we would see again, if we trained our breathing voices. it was one of few choices. and it only did what it did. and lord knows some were afraid to believe you. why? but anyway. we are still singing.[4]

from here i can see the whales, sense the whales coming. know which ones will beach themselves home to us. know which ones will go back out deep to work. it is not for me to know their choices. it is not for me to know their process. it is not for me to go and seek them. it is for me to trust. there is something deeper. something older. sometimes it gives itself to us so we can live.

from here i can see them working. i see the boats. i smell the oysters. i hear the breaking of the shells. i hear them talking into rhythm. from here i know the secrets from the tremor of the casting down of shells. and that under there is holding. from the hold the held and knowing. that these boats hold more still. more than they can tell. you get me. more than they would sell.

from here i hear the creaking. hear the old and working leaking. hear the whole half-hearted seeking neighborhood. from here i see the taking and the sacrifice and making and the tenuous and shaking and the good. from in here i hear you hoping that the working way is open. that the guides are half awake and half asleep. from here i feel you knowing that my listening is growing i am learning what to say. and what to keep.[5]

Boda

totorobonsu made the world by breathing. totorobonsu made the world with sound reaching out, bouncing back. totorobonsu moved through depths unseeable. darkness with no beginning and no end. though i am nothing, totorobonsu is now. here.

boda remembered the whale god. boda remembered the whale was god. boda remembered the world was made by breathing. boda remembered what the whales already knew. and breathed.

by the time she reached the other side she had been reborn. birthed through the belly of the whale. blue from the blood of breathing. brave from the only deep. there it was. the depth of herself. ocean. the black of her self. god.

boda made herself by breathing. by being totorobonsu in the deep. boda became. old as ocean. wise as whale. black as undrowned sun. bold as what we been through. totorobonsu. put your forehead in the water. she will show you. here i am.[1]

it was hibiscus that gave her decision. was it in dominica or san domingue or after she reached the small coral island made of volcanic wish. it was not a major port. the name of the place was for her not as important as the recognition she found in one familiar flower. it was not that the flower itself was beautiful. though it was beautiful. it was not that the flower was flagrant evidence of life spreading itself across the air. though all flowers are exactly that. it was also not that hibiscus was her favorite flower before. because she hadn't been that type of person. to favor one flower for some particular quality. or maybe she had, but at this point everything had been taken. and there was no space in that moment for particular preference. there was just the stark before and the naked now. there was the sudden and still striking meaning of skin. there was shock. it was all she could do to let blood flow into her brain. it was all she could do to let her lungs volunteer to take more air. it was a numbness that taught her to re-member that before, when she thought she knew what pain was, she had been wrong. it was the feeling that she must have been wrong to have been taken, even more wrong to have survived and unforgivable now that she had arrived.

it would be ridiculous to say that looking at a hibiscus flower healed all that. it didn't. it wouldn't work to compare the thickness of blood, the distance of salt, to the thin light touch of that flower. even of all the flowers. because the beauty of the land had already caused so much harm. and made her captors want to stay here without farm or reasonable future. it was not hope that the hibiscus gave. it was just a decision. to keep on making breath.

there are 679 species of hibiscus. trumpeting around every tropical zone of the planet. easily potted and grown even in relatively tem-perate climes. and she didn't know that. she wasn't meditating on the commonness of the extravagantly beautiful. or feeling grateful despite everything to be in a world where extravagant beauty was so common. that wasn't how it went.

it was just that she saw hibiscus. and she had seen hibiscus before. and in that moment she knew that whatever made her capable of making breath was not specific enough to be lost. was not anything that had been taken when she herself was took. it was something else. not necessarily beautiful, but available. something she could still recognize in herself. something not yet killed by space or salt air or careless hands or cruel. it was when she realized, no matter how it looked, and how it hurt and how it was small. no matter how it was threatened by tradewind and was tonic and bitter. no matter how it cleaned you out of what you wanted to keep, and so made you unclean. something continued. or maybe she remembered how cleansing it could be to be bitter. how gorgeous as it grew. how red. long story short, it reminded her that there was still something she knew. she had not choice, but decision. and she would use it to make breath. to make death. to make all of us.[2]

the first tea she made took all the flowers she could find. crushed and staining her fingers. brighter than blood and for the right reasons. she made it because she needed more than salt on skin and tracks left by what had been scraped away. she made it because maybe she would have liked to have been marked by the blood of all she had lost already. she made it as a tonic to clean out the insides meaning womb and stomach yes, meaning throat still unhealed from screaming. but also meaning heart. the organ and the part that you couldn't physically touch, but which had been touched and wounded nonetheless and trampled in the journey. it was holding the smell of the hold. she could tell.

can the petals dye the inside. already red. could she layer red over the red of what happened. over the already red of the linings of blood and muscle and not enough fat anymore. could she paint a transparent warning for the centuries of skinny children to come. could she say something by the simple act of boiling. the complicated act of breathing. the necessary act of drinking the tea in its full bitter without the sugar or honey the generations would later crave and take for granted. could she make a passage through. if not clean then at least clear. could she tell them something about life. that it was what it was. that it would stain you and screw up your face and you would still do whatever you could do. like crush every flower, not in vengeance but from need. to drink down the plants, not from thirst but from kinship. to clear out this flesh for what else could come through.[3]

there was a way the flour fell sometimes that told her. there was a quiet whisper. maybe her grandmother, she thought. there was the rain when it came. it told her when he would be by, and how to prepare.

the whales themselves would call out sometimes. sometimes the shells would break a certain way and point. and the fire. sometimes the fire would show her which way to look.

sometimes she snuck to the caves to listen. once she saw it clearly in the clouds. usually a rock or two would be enough to tell her what. and how.[4]

did you ever think about it? my name meaning wedding in the soft language of our first captors. what it justified. what it did as spell within me. for them it meant their god would justify everything they did. everyone they hurt. every carnal sin on the waiting body of the unsaved. every saving savagery they used to get us here. for them it meant what they did was blessed by god and earlier unions.

for me it meant there are some things fused together that can never be separated. sisters. despite hell and ocean. purpose. despite hell and ocean. destiny. despite everything. for me. it meant remember the ceremony. what is done cannot be undone. for me. it meant remember the journey. what i been through cannot be taken from me.

for you. it means the body stays open. a vessel itself. what i went through. for you. it means home. being it, yourself. what i lost. for you. it means presence, not patience but breathing. what i learned after all this time. for you. it means prophecy. listen to what i tell you in dreams. i will be the one in the white dress.[5]

Anguilla

they say that once the island herself had legs. and had to close them. had to bury them deep under volcano and rock. once, they say, the island herself had arms and had to arm them. with sea urchin spikes and coral edge like glass. they say what was once the belly of this island is now a place of rough scrub and hesitant green. they say once this island would swim but now she don't move at all. they say she once had long strong legs, but the small people made the sea unsafe for small reasons. if you dive deep enough, maybe you will see it. the black that she needed to protect.[1]

a volcano. a mountain in the ocean. hot. connected to the core. emerges and burns into islands. feeds coral. that's where they took us. where breathing underwater meets the fire within.

and once there, rocks. bones. shells. everything broke until it could seem soft and sharp at the same time. until it could get in through pores and poverty and screens and wood. until it could get into the food the air the traveled history.

and on the shoreline nothing. not much. nothing, but a patch you clear of burrs and pricks to get baptized. and all the buildings in the middle where the dry dust called for rain.

and in the valley, the money and the sun scorched myth of safety and the lightskinned people of ten names taking each other again and again.

and on the skin, the salt of centuries. and in the spit, the salt of centuries. and in the blood, the salt of centuries, the tears. we require a story not measured in years. begin[2] there was an empire, but that was not first. there was something else that would later be called the earlier empire. but there is no empirical data to suggest that the earlier ones would have thought of themselves in any of the terms in which the empire thought of thought. in fact, all the archaeological evidence suggests not. that the earlier inhabitants were not in the habit of settling land like it was not god. of separating god from god like god was not you. of ignoring natural law like it would bend to any lie.

meaning there were no earlier inhabitants. not in the sense that the later empire would use to claim the land for lust and slavery, but in another sense that requires all your senses to reclaim. before there was land and lust and breathing turning into dust and killable people in god's dull trust. there was us. there was only us. meaning water and blood and bone and stone and sun and change and we remain. outlasting everything.[3]

this is how we did it at the time. first thing the boats. we carved the boats. we were the boats. we were the trees.

later there would be a boat called "the tree," to sail in the races. a boat named for that tree they still gather around. because. all is not forgotten.

so those of us who got in the boats had already committed to open our bodies to salt and prayer. to pray with fire and water and hands. to pray with fish and grapes and sand. to pray with everything we were. to pray with everything we had.

that same land. unownable, realistically unknowable, for us, it was a place of prayer. of being under the ocean while breathing on land. of bringing our questions and our children. everything we wanted to understand.

so like you we used sunlight and water. we used shells and stones. we used words and touching, but this was not home. this was the place where the portal opened and closed around us, where we blessed each other as loved. where we bowed to the ocean beside us, the ocean beneath us, the ocean above. and our dead danced all around us. because because. because because. you are hoping for a special occasion, but for us, it just was.[4]

first there was the spark. a core hunger expressing itself as heat. a mountain outgrowing itself with lava. a waiting coral chorus raptured.

then there was the waiting and the sediment of cooling and the crawling and the finding that is still going on. and the tides and the truth they can't help but keep dragging in.

then there were the people who had listened for the hunger, for the spark, for the heat, for the growing lips of god. and they went into the caves because they had no shame about what they wanted. they wanted to be held, heard and reborn. so they would leave and then come back and let the tide tell them what else they should leave behind in the waiting wanting womb.

then there were the other people. who went wild with the hunger, with the spark, with the flash, with the cash economy of denial. children, dressed in the manner of nothing that has anything to do with this. so-called men who wouldn't admit that their longing for the boat was the same as their longing for the grave. the ones who would enslave and engrave pretending they didn't want to be reborn.

then there were the enslaved. the dragged away, the misbehaved whose rebirth was stole in waves, who did not ask for this. the ravaged, the brave, the initiated, the sprayed, the ones who ultimately stayed. we are still ravenous.[5]

blame the boats. the small boats tilted by wind. the large boats steeping in sickness. blame the land. blame the land for rising up so far. for cooling for climbing like thorns. blame the volcano for erupting in the first place right here. right here. right here. how could you. witness coral, microbes, and eels. how could you, you trade wind gods. how could you let them come and steal and take and forsake and bring and bind and shackle and blind and hold and hide. how could you.[6]

well, think about it. if you live on an island or a continent on a planet big like this one, how do you know the edge of the planet. why would you differentiate the ocean and outer space by something other than thickness and the type of ship?

please don't be confused and think that we didn't know the stars, the navigation strategies, the true size and differentness of the galaxies. in fact we knew we know we still look up and know about conversations between the ocean and the sky that the captors never admitted to overhearing. the yacht owners deny it to this day. is there something that keeps them from knowing? we can't speak to that.

it wasn't that we thought our village was the whole world. it wasn't that we were provincial about skin. it was what they wanted, what they did and what they tolerated, that let us know they could not be of the worlds (terrestial or celestial) that we knew.[7]

out there by the edge they draw monsters. they draw dragons into life with their lust. they make wisps of wind and waiting, they turn water into the end. there is a safe place and then there is crossing over. there is god's dominion and then there's the other place. that's how they drew on the maps they had, the ones we never had time to trace.

what we learned was that there were not neither. neither safe place nor dragons to be found. and we were only looking for the first. we were only hoping to last. we learned that there don't be monsters here. only hunger and depth. only salt and sound.[8]

we focused on the ways we were not each other. so as not to feel redundant. so as to feel only manageably accountable for each other. we used tribal origins if we remembered and then we remembered that our beliefs said we were not separate. we used surnames until those all tangled and the fathers had left. we used skin tone and reach of hair, but it didn't work. we couldn't stop reaching for each other. what's a pronoun after all of this. after not drowning after being ripped away after centuries on a tiny island building boats and salting the region. after all that could i really look you in your face and not be you?[9]

here is the story we tell. we were slaves long ago. long ago. some of us were slaves. we think more about how we were not. who white among us and whatnot. and then one great august we were free and we jumped up and so we still jump up again every august to remember. and then after we were free we were still oppressed and the sub-colony situation really didn't give us space to be men to be free for real to claim this land where we were not native but had to pretend to be because of the stories we still cannot tell. so then we were free again. every may we jump up about that. we talk about the founding fathers of our country and not the mothers. we have worked very hard to fit them into the model of other countries whose stories crowd ours out. because after all this time we still think revolution means american even though we don't say it. we don't even think it, it's just that they have already colonized that word. and we still play at freedom as our very own colony. we still play at freedom with our foreign-owned bank shares. we still play at freedom with our sun-burn-based economy. we still tell the story in the way we were taught.

the story we are not. telling. is a story rounder. more resounding. like the ocean to itself. swelling like the everyday changes that re-peat. that we meet willing or not. the story we don't tell is of being bought. of being slaves to ourselves. of being lost into salt. of violence and vault far away. the story we don't tell is the story we eat. it's the story we stomach. it's the shuffle of our feet down parade routes. the quietest stories are as loud as birth and not as old as earth though it feels so. we don't love the story about how we got here though. we can't speak the complexity we are. so we stay and make a narrative that makes us able to make it. or we go. far.[10]

we could never truly leave. we could never truly stay. we could never wait to leave. when we were gone we couldn't wait to get back. and then there was the way wind carried us. our children, our lovers on different islands. there was the food cooking up right on the beach waiting. there was the way words seemed to travel faster than wind sometimes. there were also the things we didn't want to hear.

so we became builders of boats. racers of bright sailboats. poets and painters with the names of our boats. listeners and conspirators with wind. we became arched bodies in the tilt of making landing. we became muscled approximations of freedom. roped enunciations of speed.

now every holiday, really every chance we get, we race sailboats around the island, and from every beach they watch. the compelled get in speedboats and follow us, the devoted still cooking and swimming in wait. and we still going around the question. home?[11]

tamarind and prickly pear created they us. pigeon peas and rice brought in and replanted. sea grape and hibiscus reminded us thus of color and sweetness and salt into staying. standpipe and trench maintained by whom sometimes and burr grass and crab remained. and burr grass especially came back after everything and traveled also everywhere and made itself known. burr grass unforgettably clung and climbed sideways beyond wherever it first was grown. burr grass and mosquitoes, the quiet protectors, collectors of offerings of small blood and skin. may we be like the burr grass, unforgiving future. may we be like the burr grass disdained but not ignored. may we be like the burr grass, the early and lasting. may we be like the burr grass in proliferation, in pluck, from starburst and stuck. may we be like the burr grass for the sake of our kin.[12]

love bugs and starfish they gave us them. conch and turtles too. calling birds and pelicans, jelly fish and lobster. we need them. we need what they do. mites and whales. we needed them all to teach us illusions of size. hibiscus and palm we needed them too to stop us from trusting our eyes. longing and sweetness we needed all that to shape our days into song. and wind herself slapping us with water. we needed the storms to grow strong.[13]

there were witnesses. sea grape leaves, burr grass, pelicans, actual eels. there were vines and spines for everything you did, reflectively overgrown. brutally cut down. there was nothing here that was not you and what you did to who you thought wasn't you. it's true. nothing went unseen, even in the unlit dirt roads of night. even underwater or in caves. nothing went unseen or undreamed in the short long lifetimes of the enslaved. nothing is unknown. you. don't take nothing to your grave. except maybe bones. and even those will be repurposed for limestone soon. there is no permanent space for doom or gloom, only growth. and the green, brown life around you, sees everything.[14]

what did we learn from the turtles? maybe a better question is what did the turtles learn from us. turtles could teach you about colonialism. turtles know centuries of leaving and coming back and about how when you come back and nothing is the same you wonder whether it's worth it to lay eggs or love anything. what turtles learned to do under colonialism was to die. a soft body in a hard context. a system that will stick you in your smoothest softest place, wrench you from the armor of your home. boil you and eat you like you wanted it.

and us. we made everything from turtles. the best soup in the world, and the bowls to eat it from. we made clothing, tools and pretty things to look at. it looks like you can see half the world, the distance the turtles travel, the balance they keep.

but what we learned from colonialism was to take without giving back. was to eat without gratitude.

what the Arawak learned from colonialism
was a critique we eventually ignored:

    1 that is not how you eat your gods.
    2 this is really no place to live.[15]

what the salt said.

listen. salt will steal. salt will steal the water out of your skin and the patience out of your lips if you let it.

think of what they call it. salt. mine.

did they tell you about the time we became salt. not for look back, not from leaving, but from staying. or being staid, or being slaves. not being paid. not at the beginning and not really ever enough, truth be told.

there is a type of person who will force the water to give up its salt, all day long. and they will do it with your body. let your skin peel and your sides scream. who will blind you, bind you, scour your organs for profit until you really wonder whether it is better to be the scoured or the coward.

which is which. which comes first. the salt or the water. the burning or the blessing? the pond gives you your edges and your battlegrounds. your stench and your bird sounds. your need to differentiate. your state.

and the ocean. never far away never forgetting the pond as her own. won't hear it. she says it's better to have never known. she says you can't farm what was never grown.

or here. the salt tells you itself:

leave me alone.[16]

what the seaweed kept.

nails and hair. gems and metal. everything shiny lunged for by barracuda and dropped. the leavings of baby nurse sharks. their first teeth. bones and bracelets. long since unbraided rope. held out hope for undrowned possibilities. safety for the small enough. snack bar for the greedy. sand which knew itself before as glass as shell as pearl as cartilage. there were names for some of these things before the tangle and the growing over. quiet dance of ransom. the sleeping weave of knots. the shelter of the dark in all this sun. the knowledge or the sense to root in somehow and keep hold.[17]

what the coral said.

once. we were all singing. somewhere. we are still. moving. as some-
thing huge, vibrational, wet. we dance and keep the world in place.
we shiver and know the orbit. if you let the body undulate you will
remember. not all the waves are in the ocean. we don't know so much
about the soloists. we don't know so much about virtue. we don't
care so much about your body. it's *the* body. you are already part of
it because *you* has nothing to do with it. dance into harmony now.
now is already now. time has nothing to do with it. time is up. time
is over. we are love in all directions. come on, sing.[18]

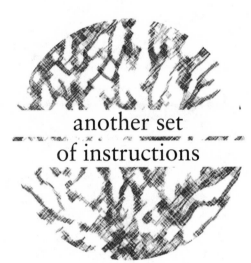

another set
of instructions

we are asking you to trust your hands. put them on your heart. trust your heart. hear what we are saying. trust what you hear. we are asking you to build a circle. always a circle. not almost a circle. face each other. we are asking you to trust the faces. face the truth. it's round. we are asking you to make a sound. make the sound you need by breathing. make the sound that calls us in. we are asking you. not telling you. listen. we will not yell. well. not yet.[1]

if you can use both hands, use both hands. knowing is not given; it is made. you can make it out of cornmeal or flour, preferably. out of dirt or fertilizer if you have to. let your fingers shape it until they remember the making of the world. then step on it. and see how easily it flattens, how gracefully it changes its shape in the presence of pressure. and remember that there are billions of feet. there is always pressure.

let the muscles in your hands grow more swift more sure from re-making it every day. a curved place to live on indented by teeth, crumbled by dryness. moisten it with what you have. spit and tears. smooth it out with what you have. repetition and patience. soon you will not have to look at what you are doing. you will feel every imperfection. you will accept some of them. you will even love some difficult edges. you can watch the river go by. you can look at the TV while you do it. maybe even have a conversation (though it will impact the consistency of your shape). but if you can. use both hands.[2]

take your hand off your forehead and remember you can already fil-
ter sunlight. take consistent deep breaths and surrender for you are
moon. let the rage held in any of the muscles in your shoulders, re-
lease. give love room.

drink enough water to remember how long water's been waiting. eat
enough plants to remember what water can do. let the fear in your
hands go back where it came from. clean the room.

call the people you've been thinking about calling. do the things your
pummeling heart says do. let the lessons forming lesions be less real
to you than children. make room.[3]

ultimately your children will forget. the names, the places, even the tastes, the flavors, the smells, the feeling of being there. the lightness or thickness of air is changing. ultimately they will too. their skin, their way of moving, their ways of knowing of feeding of mourning, rejoicing. their ways of growing might look like nothing to you.

ultimately your children will remember. the sounds, the setting, the faces, even the waste, the saving grace, the hells, the peeling of breath from air. the rightness or wrongness, the glare is wide ranging. ultimately they will do. their kin, their ways of smoothing, their ways of sowing, of feeling, of morning choices. their ways of glowing you might recognize.[4]

dig down star until you find the water. mine the water. mind the water. mine. the water waiting in you. dig down dream until you find the river. find the salted brackish liver, find the giver, find the gifts. find the guilt. find the rifts. running rivulets, the spit. the snot, the not willing to get. don't forget. dig down star, until you find the ocean. mind the notion that it's calm. find the potion, find the balm. my star dig down until tears come up. don't get stuck inside your charm. these are my arms, your shaking lungs. this is the way. these broken rungs. stretch out your bones, starfish. become.[5]

stomp until it become dance. stomp until it be. come dance. wake us with your feet. we live in your hips. wake us with your hips. we live in the ground. keep dancing (with the wake in your waist) and follow. we will tell you where to go.

cleanse. your sweat an offering. your salt a memory. your return to water, long. awaited. wash like no one's watching. wash like everyone's waiting. wade like you know trouble. where it waits and how it watches. drink from upstream.

stack them. stack your sisters. stack your sayings. stack the stolen stuffy days. stack the secrets. stack the staying. and stand back. look at the cost. long for the lost. scream as loud as you want. and curse like a prayer. braid it into your hair. let it cut through the air, and your fingertips. put your hands to your lips, to remember the blood. okay good,
now scream as loud as you should.

put your hands on your belly and breathe. keep your hands on your belly and grieve.
with both hands on your belly leave. all your best things. behind. leave all. your blessed things. besides your hands. put your hands on your belly. let it grow. and let go. and know.

burn it out. bleach it out. leach it out onto the counter. cook it into cake. make more than you can take. and more than you can keep. refuse to weep. forget to sleep. wake up to pray. clean out the day with rum and rose water. grow hibiscus and daughter where it is said they should not grow. burn and know.

help until you can't help it. help until you hurt. hurt until you can't heal any more.
then work. work until you can't worry. work until you can't wait. work until you get weary with wisdom and hate. hate until you can't

hear it. hate until you can't not. hate until you hear whispers. listen until you get caught. catch until you catch feelings. catch until you catch up. lift until you find feelers under the muck. muck until you make meaning. mean until you make more. move until you can't mean it.
then sit down at the door.

sit. and the singing surrounds you. sit in the steady screams. stay and listen behind it all for the stars and the whales and the dreams. stay for the songs that find you. stay for the smallest sound. stay your behind right here and sit directly on the ground.

open your mouth.

now give us what you found.[6]

red august

what i did not do? disappear. burn up. flake away. with or without the name. what i did? stay. and outlive the makers of that name. do you hear me? i wore this hair into ash from a flame and i used every single thing my grandmothers knew about the blood of a fire-drinking man.

what i went through? it's too simple to name. too usual to claim. it was every single day. it was meant to be this way. it was what heat did and what cruelty could not take away. it was my lot. which does not mean it was not too much. but it lived in the place between strike and touch. and it touched you eventually. i know that.

what i knew? i knew soft and rough. i knew twelve spaces of voice, above and below each of the children. i knew salves and waiting. i knew other words for love. i knew you. in your stubbornness. in your brightness. in your quiet. i knew there was something else waiting in the enough.

what i did? i gave and i slid. i kept and i hid. i forgave and reneged. i did everything. i did low and out of sight. i did before daylight. i did must and did might. i did everything right. but they don't think so.

and my name? hurricane not of sugar, of time. fierce mother of all nine. season of change. granddaughter of luck, granddaughter of range. you know my name. and i know yours.[1]

at some point it was her and her children. out in the sun baking. up before the sun making bread. wearing clothes made of flour sacks.

before that it was her with the other children. skinny. skin growing hard against the salt here. the men she knew not new to starvation, not sure if their legs were for island or ship.

before that then was the frozen ground. the frozen ground and the persistent rot. the persistent rot and the well-traveled hunger. at least by the land standards of the people who ate potatoes.

before that there must have been green and there must have been brown and there must have been blue but they called her red. and she baked like the bread. on purpose.[2]

first time i tasted dirt, i knew it was medicine. the very first time. i was too young to speak. but *look what it does for the potatoes* i said in my mind. i wanted to always be in it. i wanted it on me. i loved it more than water. they could never wash me clean. what did it mean? it meant i brought something of my country along with us. and then what happened with Augusta, they blamed me.[3]

dirt. it was dirt i remember of home, and not enough of it where we landed. not enough to hold me together. when we got there it was sun and air so warm you could hold it. hug it while you held yourself together. that's what i often did. there is a difference between hard ground and coral. a difference between shale and post-volcanic fossils. the others thought there was dirt enough to stay. land enough to make home here. and it wasn't up to me. for them i was a place of clean enough and useful. for them i was a way of making future out of loss. if when we landed you would have told me i would have a red granddaughter like Gussie. who would love it here and never dream of green. i wouldn't have been able to stomach what you mean. and you? my grave. forget about it.[4]

imagine a hedge. there is no hedge. the soil could never support it. imagine a fence. the salt would rot it. imagine the height of the house of his marriage and the lowness of the shack of his lust. and then remember they all lived on the same hill. there is no configuration of windows. there is no angle of yard that shades out the shame. he had children with his wife and his neighbor. and others for sure. and you? you come from next door.

maybe the neighbor hung clothes on a line to divide them. the sackcloths she used to cover her children. the evidence of poverty and industry like flags. that couldn't have helped. someone said once that the wife and the neighbor (i didn't say mistress) were actually very good friends all along. they understood something no one else could understand. someone most other people couldn't stomach. did they share salve for bruises. everyday tonics for when he drank too much. did they add anything to the process that ultimately shriveled his liver to nothing, his living to children building strive out of hurt.

there was no wall. nothing like that at all. and they were not close enough to the sea to block out any sound. and there was sound. when he was around. and the children to manage. playing out politics without a stable border. so whatever they did not see. whatever they chose not to see, was held in the tense corners of their necks. their eyelids swift enough to look down before one could be sure they had seen what they could not speak against. their very different hair sometimes strategically placed to veil them.

you know this well enough in your neck. well in your shoulders. you wake up stiff unlearning all the truth that can't be said. for you are still the neighbor. brazen and next door to structure. you are right next door with all the pride of the displaced. you are all night dreaming that you won't wake up to screaming. subtle muscles for a day that you can't face.[5]

hear her say chueps. hear her say get down from there boy you gwan fall and knock your teeth out. hear her say the same things but sound different because her teeth go one by one. hear her say go. go i can't stop you. hear her say try this, put your foot through here. hear her say wake up sweetie or i gone. hear her say watch the bread rise don' touch yet. hear her say touch wood. hear her knock on the floor and not say anything. hear her say you just like ya fada. but not to you. hear her say rain soon comin' after singing something in a language you don't know. and when you ask her, hear her say she don't know what those words mean either but her grandmother used to sing them and they didn't work because the ship still land here and break out on those rocks so. but it wasn't the song that was wrong, you know. it's not the words why i'm singing it. it's just when i sing it she here. i here. her voice.[6]

somebody told me they carry their own gods in their pockets. is that true? and what if god is small like that. i don't know. i wasn't taught much about that. but i could believe in a god that could fit in my own hands. that's what i had to believe in raising those kids. my own hands empty and working. moving and making. the help the size of what someone could put in my palm discreetly, or their own hands helping out. my hands lined on both sides with roads and rivers to possibility. the pathways i would focus on. the purpose of these hands to keep those children alive. when i think about it now, what did i believe in more? the cross in church or the crossing and crossing over, the scars and sacrifices of these hands. would have been sweet to have a nice small god to put in my apron pocket those days. as long as the children wouldn't choke on it or throw it away. as long as no one had to see it but me? sure.[7]

can you multiply? let me tell you the shape of it. his father had swam free from sharks, they say, to marry his mother, a Fleming. or to prevent someone else from doing the same. they say she was very beautiful then. anyway, he overcame drowning to pass on the name. to a son.

and then that son. at least one, because there were in fact others. drowned the name in drunken desperate seeking. Gumbs. in violence and in weeping. in brazen company keeping. and everyone pitied my friend, his wife. but i was not even the wife. i was other company kept.

and company keepable because Brooks had died and left me with two children to raise alone. and it was the drunken wreck that gave me seven more. i became mother of nine. in the end none of them really his, in the end all of them mine. but the name persisted. Gumbs. soaked in knowing and silence.

do you understand? and before that i had already been rejected by the Carty clan for choosing to choose an African man. Brooks. and for choosing a lifetime of sidewise aunt and grandaunt looks. because they had hoped for generations burnt and not brown. and we didn't love each other that much after all. and i didn't feel something at home i wanted to keep feeling. even though i let them keep calling me Carty, after father. so already reeling from being disowned, and then sort of widowed and then scorned and then visited by a drunk and raging man again and again, i learned the shape of being in the exponential world of men and names. being without a way to say that i was here. but i won't let you let them forget me. i won't let you let them let me. i won't let you let me disappear.[8]

sleep? what about sleep? do you think children care if you sleep? and their father? maybe it was to respect his wife's sleep that he stayed the nights he stayed. maybe it was to get some sleep away from that house. i didn't ask.

yes. i slept like a whale. one part of my brain always alert to drowning. i always heard when he crept in. i always heard when he crept out. yes. i slept like the shipwrecked granddaughter i was. the soothing depth of water can kill you. there are rocks and coral all through here. if i slept. i slept like a mother of nine. you've started to know what this feels like. all the parts of you, outside your body but close. and the listening that doesn't stop. and the rudeness of their own ups and downs. and the impossibility of turning it off. so yes. sometimes i woke up crying and couldn't say why. but at some point i didn't really wonder. you learn this on an island. you learn this when a shipwrecked people raise you. you learn this from the sweat of an island man. you learn. from the snot of your beautiful children. the salt water is there, in any form to claim you. so no. i never really slept.[9]

when first did i know i couldn't tell him nothing. could only show. could only be. must be when he fought him father. told him father he would starve if the food came from his dirty hands. age. maybe 10? he did it to protect me. but he somehow couldn't hear me there screaming. begging him to stop. hoping and hoping not that the neighbors would hear and know everything that they already had been knowing. he couldn't hear me then. and he heard me but didn't listen when i told him not to get on the boat. because i knew what a boat could do. break. i knew what leaving could mean. forever. who was i. only his mother. red and shipwrecked on dry and yellow land. but those who cannot hear will feel anyway. i mean what can i say. what do you really want me to say? with what i knew about men? i had a youngest son who would do anything for me. except do what i say. and since when were you so obedient anyway?[10]

when the children don't eat, their stomachs get round with gas. they hold it. the emptiness of the planet. i hold it. the helplessness of a woman who cannot after all feed them the rocks that are left. no matter what they tell you, i didn't want my son to leave with his cousin when the sharks came around looking for cheap workers so they wouldn't have to pay the dignity cost of the Tingo rebels. the planet is empty. i know that. but gas, like everything else, moves. and it hurts when it moves and it pushes on the organs. i know that from my own childhood. the smaller the organs the sharper the pain. the more vulnerable the bones. the more angry the disrespected impulse saying "grow." he had to go. i know that. he was proud and didn't know that he could die. i was tired and i knew that he could. i also knew death would have an even harder time with him than his father did. that kid could fight. would fight anything. would fight with anything he had. and in my house he had almost nothing but me.

when he came back he told me about the bull who gored, the strangers who healed, the cold cold ground and his small weak ankles. but only after he handed me the money after handing some to the man to make a suit. that little boy would say "suit" like he could taste it, candy in his mouth.

when he came back again he told me about the high towers in the oil fields and the flame he had to light at the top. a gas flame that had to stay lit and he was the only one small enough to scramble up. *a gas flame?* i asked. *a gas flame. it always has to stay lit.* he repeated. *yes.* i nodded. *i know about that.*[11]

this is what you do when the world is too dry for breastmilk. when you cannot feed your children on your tears. when the ocean is rising up around you and within you and breaking all your breathing into splinters. you stop. you don't have a day to alchemize grief into calcifications of the arteries, inflamed veins in vain. you have three minutes before one of these children wakes up. there are roosters everywhere. so you turn yourself immune to all the names for this. you hold your face tight and breathe quiet as a leak. you turn it into leather, face the sun. you turn your face in time to move uninterrupted. you turn your face into a map folded. creased by the not finding, dusted by the not looking. you draw your face like curtains, not a bath. the world is too damn dry.[12]

i practiced. looking into the faces of my sisters. until it didn't hurt anymore. until any wrinkles from squinting at the sun became laugh lines. i struggled. to put my hands in the fire until even coals became cool and no surface could hurt me again. i persisted through pregnancy and birth until i knew. i knew creation. i did it nine times and then i was eternal. you know what i mean. notice the challenge. notice the discomfort. notice how many times you want to run away from you and us and everything. notice. and do not stop.[13]

it's true, there is a certain light. a certain unjustifiable glow around a person. an unearned shine, you could call it that. when i saw him it was as if the sun or moon was in the right position, lighting the parts of him that would call me. hiding the parts that would have made me run away for just long enough. almost long enough.

lighting is everything.

so you say you are with a *filmmaker*. a person who makes stories with light and what can be shown. a person who changes the world with what is visible and what is held off in the shadows. i can understand that. yes. i know something about that.

and i offer you my blessing. actually i already did. all i ever wanted was to be part of some people dedicated to light on purpose, offering all their darkness to the making of possible. all i wanted was all that held back love, that distorted reshaped denied love to have its day. congratulations.[14]

no one ever asked about the moment of her skin against his skin. about how the first time he held her hand she saw stars framed against the sky, her self bound bracing the universe. she was visible, not against sand, but against him, darker than stone, enveloping. instead of breaking to red, she could find brown in him. fertile. she could make brown through him. she could hold brown worlds within become round like the planet should be. all those mornings with the bread she would think about it. remake it. actually bake it. the white becoming brown. the flour becoming earth to feed the workers. she would teach her children to aspire to brown. to float towards brown. that the tendency was to move, to rise towards brown, forever brown, to leave behind the paleness and grow brown. so unlike the other people in their town who prized white skin and transparent eyes, her sons, who agreed on almost nothing else, gravitated towards dark brown women with their eyes in books. earth women even if they were in outerspace. the good birth, she taught them is brown is brown is brown. and now she looks at her generations, stardust against their blackness and offers the heat of the oven at dawn, clear against the coolness of time. offers the patience and attention of a woman who literally made bread out of stone, rock oven. made love out of what some would have called nothing. she bakes it into them as the sun itself rises. a memory that god is good and brown.[15]

you know about it. where they don't have to make you die, they can just let you die. god already salt the land now they put pepper in the soup. have you living on a small island like it's the big world of diverse markets. most of the men here can't even find enough spots to put their pitchfork and must travel to several other islands for plant, if you get my meaning. why, if you put a road here, would it work like a road on a big island like England? i make a son with the same hate love for England i have. like an allergy to dust in this dry place. or hay fever in a barn. whatever. whatever is the least they let happen over there, we here make life with even less than that.[16]

you want to know what it was like to give birth here? we would envy the whales. those long-carrying mothers birthing underwater, singing all the while. we would have to squat on land and pray there was someone to sing around us. we would have to make our own water, offer our blood and tears. remember water from before, visualize rainy years and other places. other women would come around to help with the other children even if you were (like i was) the other woman. even the other other women would come help. we all thought these children were worth it, because of or despite these worthless men.

it was a holiday. not because life ain' hard. or 'cause labour ain' work but because these babies don't care what time of day or night they have you stopping. because somebody got to clean the whole house like it's Christmas. because if they a boss that decide about the timing of this birth thing, that boss ain' no man.

and you know. round the clock bond of this birthing thing. this showing up and opening up. the holding of hands and all of us crying about something that may have nothing to do with this child or this day, was a more important bond after all than the snuck or churched combining with the menfolk who stayed and left and left their names or money or not at all. so when you ask how we could be friends and neighbors even knowing our men were moving all around and betwixt and between it was because when someone holds your hand, washes your floor, covers you in the yard, brings the tea left over from her time, stands in the doorway with you while you see the edge of all that is possible and come back from it breathing, while you open past the open of open into the splay of never the same, everything else between you and that woman is small and fall through, like the daily promises of men who forgot they were there too in the anytime black of birth once.

those of us who have been in the face of birth together, we can forget anything but that. we can forget everything in fact. we must forget everything but that witness. and who else knows.[17]

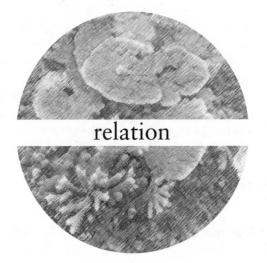

relation

in the middle there was the longing. salted. kept for him. and never enough water. even (especially) in the middle of the ocean.

in the middle there was the loss. kept from her. preserved in the same liquor that corroded its edges. sharp to the liver. to the living in general.

in the middle there was the wound. kept from them. persistent need to cover over. scab of never sweating. doing everything right.

in the middle there was the knowing. kept for us. blurred access at the edge of dreams. gut breathing underneath the wails. taste for it. and know.[1]

prophet

bricks are flat and shells are sharp and rock is whatever shape it is broken. and cement will fill or crack the spaces in between. the thing about this wall is that every piece is different. you don't get into a rhythm. you turn each piece around in your hand. like how the truck keeps turning the cement into concrete. you wonder one time whether god is doing just that with the planet, turning it around in his hand a few million times to consider how best to build something else altogether. and do the mountain ridges and the needling buildings prick his palms.[1]

then they came for the children. the small fingers and large bellies of the starving children. the children marooned to islands of neglect. they came and they stole them from their mothers in the night through hunger dreams. and dreams of clothes not made from flour sacks. and dreams of dignity diluted with dollars. they came and offered dollars for the children again. they came with boats outfitted just for cargo and filled them with small knees and splintered hands. they let the babies vomit out their knowing, far from land. they took them and they put them in the middle. they used them to outwit the brash and brave. they knew there was no future for sugar without the thick technology, the slave. they made believe like this was a free market. where life was scarce and workers must compete. they took their boats to small surrounding islands. they found him. his big eyes, his blistered feet.[2]

sometimes when an island is so big you don't think of it as an island. when an island is so trade interconnected that you can get anything, you don't really think of it as an island. when an island feels so solid after you've spent a whole week vomiting on a boat, you just don't think so much about how this land is an island. at least that's how it was for me. even when i climbed high up to the flare in the oil distillery all i saw around me was land and the brown and red people. all i really felt was the smoke. and before that in the cane fields, all i felt was the numbness in my feet. the cold and then the aftercold. the feelings i would never feel again through my long walk at life. the feelings i didn't want to feel, like when that bull gored out my heart. the story i didn't want to say, like that i was in the middle of an uprising. the people still didn't want to be slaves. but i was just a little boy, a scab they got because my mother thought my father would kill me. because my mother couldn't feed me anyway. because i wanted some clothes for myself and some things for my mother. but it wasn't worth the ship that got me there. sometimes a revolution is so long you don't think of it as a revolution. but still. i never forgot.[3]

i thought if i could cut a suit by hand, i could make myself. i thought if i could cut my father out of our lives, i could make it. i thought if i could lift the world like Atlas, i could make a self strong enough not to end up like my father. i thought if i could hold my breath, i could make it. i thought if i could dive below the wreckage i helped make, i could get under it. i thought if i could clean a gun, i could aim through the soot of life. i thought if i could pivot and turn and choreograph and yell and twist and march a platoon of men in perfect formation i could get out ahead of it. i thought if i could walk far enough, i could send money home to free her. i thought if i could go far enough, the other one would forget. i thought if i came home rich they would just forget everything. i didn't come home. i thought if i sent books they would know i was smart. i thought if i sent pen and paper they would forgive me for not writing. i thought if i didn't come back they couldn't help but remember me grand. but i married a woman who taught me that the children wouldn't understand. i married a woman brave enough to go with or without me back to the land. so i thought if i bought all of us tickets the sight of home couldn't break us. i thought if i bought a whole airline we could go wherever wind wanted to take us. i thought if i hired my whole family the shaky ground of that man couldn't shake us, but it still did. what if your father is a man you don't want to talk about with your kids. what do you say then? i thought if i came home then what america did wouldn't count. i didn't count on my granddaughter moving right back to the wretched south. i thought if i taught her the poems she could at least know what i was about. let's see how this works out then.[4]

i became a machine. what did it? lifting more than i could lift. taking more than i could take. the way i wished myself steel to break my father's fist. the cold on my young ankles in the cane fields that didn't freeze me. the way i posed as Atlas, world and world-on-shoulders at once. the necessary transition from coal and ice to heaters and air-conditioners. the dive to pull my nephew from the wreckage of the plane. the many times the boats could not be what i needed. i became a machine. ask the kids. i worked the impossible. i became bolts and creaking places. that's why i needed the poems.

make me a poem about coal. about how its blackness holds the spark. about how bright it holds the heat. a computer poem about coal. how it processes what could destroy us into time. i didn't know one day i would have a long white beard. i just knew what my father-in-law knew. a lump of coal can save you. give your children one more day. black heat will stop your wanting to be white. will draw your hands regardless. make me a poem about how long it took for a green plant to become a black ignitable fuel. reborn after photosynthesis to find the sun within. make me a poem about pressure. my father-in-law's truck and daughter. my son always following behind. let me show you how in between generations we become diamonds. pressed on all sides reflecting light. how we open ourselves to rainbow, learn to cut through death, changeable only by one as strong, as pressed upon as we.

make me a poem about ice. where sweat meets rock meets breath. as i heave the unbelievable back onto the truck, lest your great-grandfather think i am weak. make me a poem about cold i would have never believed. let me teach you about a world that was harder than i could have imagined. and how i craved the liquid space to grieve. let me tell you why i had to leave. i needed water that could not freeze up on you in the light of day. depth and motion where i could be weightless and not at all strong. i needed baptism. to be reborn so many times, as plant as dirt as worry as work as stubbornness as hurt as home as you. heat your poems, cool your head, bring me through.[5]

your grandmother could throw her voice. high. over barbed-wire racists who weren't looking, only hearing and imagining their own jersey cows. sows. their sisters i mean. (i know i'm not right.) your grandmother had an educated voice that came from stealth, sweetness and separation. i loved her voice up to a point. because the woman could talk. i mean the woman could talk like it was a marathon to raise money for sick children or something. i think she had an extra source of breathing. the woman could talk without rest. do you know something about that? there was always another idea coming out pushed by the ideas behind it. like a faucet maybe, stuck on open. to the fatigue of mere mortals like me. to the joy of the ever thirsty ground.[6]

how many times did she write the letter. how many versions did she not send. how does it balance her wanting to know and not wanting to know it in the end. how many ways to phrase the question. how many things to do instead. how many secrets how many secrets, asks the howl inside her head.

this is the thing. here she is with a man who wants to become her father instead of becoming his own father and to be the father of her children, but may already be a father to a child far away. here is a person who may be father to a child but did not stay. here is a path away from her father but into her father's way. one thing you should know about Lydia though, is Lydia does not play.

she did write the letter. and at least one version got sent. and when the answer was *do not ask,* fear of heights notwithstanding, she went. pregnant with her own big secret she went to see this place. that her father's favorite suitor (now her husband) wouldn't face. ultimately they all went down there to see what exactly was true. and like every woman ever, the truth was something she already knew. the big secret wasn't a woman or child it was the depth and the lightness, the blue.[7]

what about the dogs. when loyalty mattered more than looks or speech and presence. mattered more than equality. what about the people who would have been better if they had been dogs, concerned only with being alive, with being with you and not with gain. what did you tell or show the dogs that would have been too much a test for any person, too subtle for those who could see color and make it mean. what about when dogs didn't live as long as they deserved and people were too evil to go somewhere and lay down. what about when dogs were right about who should be trusted. what about dogs that were so sweet they trusted anyone and died for it. what about the scratching, sleeping, waiting life of love that doesn't leave or lie about it.

what about the birds. what about the talking birds. what about the mocking laughs of the talking birds. what about the messages. what about the sharp mouths of birds with names of land and patriarchy. what about the rhyming names of birds. the freedom reaches of caged birds. what about the island fate of birds who cannot swim. what about the paradox of birds with brains too heavy for their wings. what about the knowing way a bird will call you out.[8]

at a certain point i was the one they didn't want. to be around. well truth be told the one they *did* want to be around in light-skinned night but not the bright of day. worse than fatherless. i was not of a family they wanted to make their own. though it was of course known that we were all family. i think they dreamt of a future where their children would be further and further away from mine. i think they are still dreaming it. some of them. wherever they are.

the irish irony of it is that the woman who taught me to love black people. who gave up kin and connection to do it, does not show up to remind these progeny of mine what it is. what it is worth. until half the time it is too late. more than half the time. so i'm here to tell you again. i was the poorest child. black child starving. black boy naked fatherless. did i say hungry. did i say last son of a single mother of many. in a colonized country starving in the salt air. don't get away from yourself and leave me. a small black boy without water. whom. you. now. need. to. love.[9]

clothes. there could never be enough clothes. he touched them. all the beautiful suits. edged next to his wife's originality and flair. he touched the shirts, the gloss of shoes. he could not decide what to wear.

he would be speaking at the graduation. everyone would be there. himself included. the tailor he had been. the barber, the smuggler, the tough reckless on a bicycle, the muscled youth carrying a chip the size of the world. all there under his clothes. and under that the boy he had been at school, naked but for a flour sack.

in the crowded school that he had organized to fund. sent remittances back home to build. to fill with shipments of books. blank paper. pencils. chalk. do they still use slates? he used to write his sums in sand. he looks at his hands. will they shake?

the heat at the graduation will be a given. even if it spills outside. and nonetheless the people will be thoroughly clothed in the thickest material they could find. dressed as much as possible like the people who don't live here. he is a person who does not live here anymore. but can they see the flour sack peeking, the naked boy with the irish mother seeking strength of more than voice. and what of the rumors and stories. have they lessened or grown from his solid choice to leave. he grieves the grief of the relieved when they show him to a seat. show him where to stand. he eats his choice to have forsaken his so-called native land. his face, facing eighteen years of children cheeky, cherished and unplanned and he does not know one of them. what is the stitch, the warp, the cut for eighteen years away. abroad as long indeed as he ever lived here. and back today for what.

there can never be enough. clothes. pencils. concrete school floor over the dirt. he takes too long to choose which crisp white shirt.[10]

you know how i felt about suits. so imagine me in my uniform. pressed and perfect. creased and crisp. decorated with buttons and bravery and the built-up blood of brethren. or so it was said. tan uniform up against my brown skin. North Carolina sun. remember how i told you about the chiggers. how they would get under your skin. well the uniform covered all of that. bites and blemishes. ash and anxiety. or so you would think. but maybe it was that exact feeling of safety. of being held. of bronze belonging blasted to the bone. that made white people hate seeing me in uniform. that wouldn't let them leave me alone.

and all i wanted to do was ride a bus. visit a family friend.

i don't know how to tell you how close every moment back then was to veritable end. it was not safer to walk. but the projectile talk of the bus driver was too much. and at least among the trees and the bugs there was dignity.

i thought it would be simple. but it was not. and with my uniform wrinkled i made it ultimately to that place. and they saw what was creased into my face and recognized it as their own. i'm trying to say it so you can know:

i hate that country. i will not live there. i hate that country. it is not my home.[11]

it was a small island. so you couldn't say that looking like someone give you the right. you couldn't say that looking like someone give you the right to walk up to me in the bank i help found and say you are my son. foundling. ask your mother. i would know as much as anyone, that having the name, the face, eventually the voice and talent for fishing don't give you any rights in the face of a man who could always disclaim being your father. ask your mother. everyone looks alike. or at least to her. ask her about me and my brother. my own wife already asked her. don't take her silence out on me. it don't give you any right.

and who do you think you are anyway. you were no more than a speck when you chased me from this island but you wait til now, when you are tall enough to look me in my face to try and shame me in front of all the people i left, all the people i came back to, including you. this is a small island. no one forgets. i didn't forget. you don't have to remind me. you don't have to remind me what it looks like to have no father. boy. i know.[12]

of an acquaintance of my grandfather named Fidel

he was of the society of men who wore uniforms and never died. they did it with live chickens from Harlem basements. they did it with the specificity of facial hair. they did it through a visual tactic of recognition so that you saw what you thought you knew and did not check for signs of decay or delayed breathing. they did it with newspapers and sound bites. they did it by saying the same thing over and over again. simply put, he let you memorize him so when his body couldn't do, so when his brain quietly fled, you would do the work for him with your beating heart, your wishing breath, your own dependable mind.[13]

if you asked the conch. the shell. if you ate the conch and kept the shell. or after all the conch soup if you picked up a shell, like the ones on top of the walls along the road, or the shined ones in souvenir shops. listen. whatever happened to the conch is happening to you too, you know. homeless. forgotten. signified only by the shell you leave. how all that calcium you ate became the teeth and hair in pictures. how interchangeable in the end. your ancient body. how soft you were inside. how spired, hollow and singing. how hard. and sharp and sounding like the ocean. sounding like yourself. the home you left behind.[14]

the hair on the top of his head went away. the pain in his ankles stayed. the body and the breathing eventually fled. the stories over-told outweighed. the poems and the prophecies kept to their trade. the land, as predicted, was whittled away. the kids rarely used the road. the conch shells sang memories no one could hear. melodies no one could play. except the granddaughter with death in her ear. who went back to offer and pray.

the teeth and the triumph trucked blunt in his face. the trek and the taxes of time. the knives in his knees could be daily replaced with the changing contour of the tides. the bay in the end where he met Father Time and Poseidon and others with beards, was the place they would come when they needed his calm to embrace them across the years. to outbalance their failure and tears. wanting *is* instead of *appears*. to relieve their pores of their fears. the ocean. that's what is still here.[15]

and

and now his skin is slack and honest, bag of silenced desperation. now his liver, cleaned of living by the proof. now his children scattered this way, that way, their way, anyway. away. wanting nothing further from him than the name and each other. now that it is only this bed. not of lust or of convenience or of as much novelty as one can seek on a small island in the middle of the week. now that it is only this bed for waiting to die. now that it is only him, bedded down by his decisions and the demons that made those decisions daily and the days that made those demons seem enough. only now does red's youngest son come back. holding the hand of his own son as though to both crow and protect.

he hears him say it whether he says it or not. he feels him spit whether he spits or not. he remembers this son at eleven years old willing to fight for an honor he himself couldn't imagine. the honor of his mother. the honor of all their mothers maybe. it made him bold. impossible. and he left and he left again. only now he comes back with a son. and he hears the little boy say, *why didn't mommy come? what about sis?* and then the answer.

when did the once belligerent boy grow gravel in his throat. when did he break off all those stones and keep them. and the answer comes and stays. the grown boy says *because this man is not fit for the sight of decent women.* and his dry dying mouth is too weak to answer, his own gut rot by rum and running, his loud mouth gummed and dumb and grave.

in his being his body says: *this is your final warning. take it or repeat me like a slave.*[1]

and they think i was mean. some thought i was reckless and stupid. others considered me a joke. the truth was i was empty and couldn't accept it. i didn't accept it. i tried to fill myself with pleasure and felt betrayed because it didn't work. i know in the story you will tell i am the betrayer, but i really believed i had nothing to give. and i gave all of it. rage and lust, i didn't leave any of it inside. i wrung my body out liver first trying and failing to be alive. i don't know how to tell you about it. talking about it to someone wasn't an option at the time. there was only access to liquor and women and wine and lime and grind and grime. and i am not saying that i can teach you something. but just know. and act accordingly. know this and act accordingly: you are not empty this time.[2]

and one more thing. there is nothing to say i was not a healer my-self. a prophet. an intuitive. whatever you would call it. you can see evidence of it in my children. in who they attracted. you can see it in yourself. and if you can believe a black woman artist would most likely end up screaming in the asylum. what do you think could happen to a black male prophet on a small island under colonialism. think about it. 'cause i'm not telling. think what could have made me the way i am. think. how i made you the way you are. and what was it made both of us. all of us before that. and at this point. are you ready?[3]

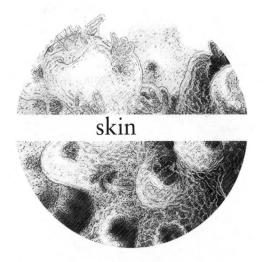

skin

she was on the coastline with her goats. walking the goats? goats do not need supervision to wander around eating everything. she was there for a different reason. her dreams. her dreams told her everything. like not to listen to the cheap advice of the fearful. like not to threaten her pulsing brain with hair-pulling. so they called her a madwoman and wild. therefore, though she freely told her dreams to the people for nothing. they paid her no mind. maybe if she had asked them to pay they would have thought about it differently. but her dreams told her it wasn't money she needed, but time. just so, she had told William Gumbs her dream. she had seen it very clearly. the rocks would tear up the boat and the sharks would eat up their bodies. and with his wedding coming up he should probably just stay home.

no. she didn't need dreams to tell her the common sense of her own people. he had already got the suit. and that pretty Catherine Fleming. and he went out fishing for a last adventure, and supposedly to bring back more fish for the party. more fish to sell for money for drinks for the party. whatever. in the dreams weddings meant death, but she knew he wouldn't listen. so she was there at that particular piece of coast when he dragged himself in, ragged, naked and bleeding. panting pantless about how his friends had died. and she took off her petticoat and let him wear it. later he would say the voice of god had given him the strength to swim all the way home chased by friend-eating sharks. later he would say it was the love of Catherine that wouldn't let him drown (or fear, others said, that she would quickly choose another). later he would even admit, that the madwoman herself had warned him with her dream. and he should have listened. some of his great-great-grandchildren would hear about that. she was quiet, since she had already said what she knew. simple petticoat over his generations. and the great-great-grands with their own wild hair? yes. she had already seen them in dreams.[1]

115

from his house he could see the port. he was the only one who called it a port. around him they were all soaking their minds in rum. his wife's cousins, he called them. though in truth they were all his cousins too. cousins at the very least. he pretended not to smell the roasting goat elevating from the barbecue barrels below. he prided himself on the shape of his nose. *distinction.* he called it, to himself because no one was listening. like how the pier makes sense of the raucous curve of shore, like how the concrete reteaches the sandy coral ground, like how he taught his wife to cook his food without pepper sauce.

so when Bradshaw said he would put pepper in the soup of the Anguillans, Emile Gumbs was offended too. but all this talk of seceding from the British Empire was too hot. to tell the whole world at that? they may as well also go live in the caves. he sat on his upstairs porch and let the salt wind come in. when the British got here they would straighten it out. and he? he would give them whatever they wanted. his name, this house, his sight. he put down his glass of gin and waited for time to prove him right.[2]

the problem was i loved them more than skin. more than yellow. more than the sun itself. more than smooth. i loved them both. that was the first problem. i loved them for no good reason. that was the older math. my mother would have said *angle?* and i would have said squiggles on paper, in the sand, ink on my hands. i would have said fingers tracing circles. triangles where the edges can't quite meet and something spills out of the open space. none of which she would have understood. or would have understood too well. so i told her nothing. my father would have said *property?* and i would have said i give myself away i give myself away. i would have said it twice a day. because maybe it was not that i loved both or either. it was not yet that i really knew love. it was more that i knew not love. i knew that my father did not love me more than fair. knew that when he was there he did not want to be there. knew it by his face as soon as he came back from elsewhere. he give himself away. *property?* he would have said. and i would have said i don't know about that. *angle?* mama would have asked as i got round. but when the baby came i knew something about my own. and keep. and how by now to be sharp on paper. when the letter came asking, was this baby his or his. i knew how to write no. and stop. and mine and only mine.[3]

he keeps the names in a book. keeps the spells in a ledger. keeps the poems in a three-ring binder with page protectors. but the keepers of memory do not keep everything. some memories do not qualify. some truths are not worthy. some known or heard legends are unspeakably dirty. so he doesn't tell me.

and yet. one day on a terracotta porch shared with cats and latticed concrete, the neighborhood grunting by in the patterned sun. he does share. what happened to him at school. what they did to him because he was black. not just black conceptually, but black visually. what they stole that could not, cannot be replaced. what jooked him in the cortex, the place of his psychic ability, total recall. he went to school and they stole his memories.

what happens when you are forced to endure something you can't bear to remember. what happens when the only way to endure is by not remembering. what happens when one day remembering becomes the only way to survive. the good news is he is still alive. and cousins come by and visit sometimes. saying things like *how are you, this is my book, i brought you a copy.*

and so one day he does say what happened. and we listen. and he says *therapy* he says *light* he says *finally* he says *night.* he says *i feel so much better.*

and that. i keep here.[4]

scientist. interested from an early age in technologies of elevation and descent for their own sake. leaves and rocks off the ground for their mere presence in his path. the possibility that the forbidden and unbought could be made from scratch. the language of hairless cats. the sounds of digital motion. the pixilated journey of the working class Italian American hero. the immigrant. the brother. the dream.

for his experiments he put rocks under his pillows and slept. collected shells from as deep as he could breathe in cups that had erstwhile held Sprite. tracked dreams where he could breathe underwater. sought to replace Sprite itself with something that could bubble with the lemons and limes at home. documented dreams where he could fly. wrote books about the adventures of small round heroes forever at battle. gave them names that said what they did. played race-car video games with the controller turned backward so forward was always toward his own heart.

he learned what he learned. what he could learn quietly. he learned what he learned. weapons and patterns and cards. he learned what he learned. which was to breathe underwater. he also learned to fly. take heed.[5]

losing it all

go to the edge. when you get there dig your heels in. step back. kneel down. lean your lungs over the ledge and scream. stomach into the void and retch. hands holding rocks. throw them. empty out. breathe. stay there. your head as low down as possible. until all you can hear is the sound of your breathing. ragged and loud. this is how you know that the edge of the world is not the end. do you know it? when you know it, turn around.[1]

because it is safer. because it would be safer. if your skin was airtight, not just some shaking sound. this body if you could just live in it, it would be simple. if you could just stay inside it and not leak everywhere. if you could just swift unnotice the forcefield around your chest. if you just weren't so black. meaning dark. like the pull of the universe expanding at the speed of itself. if you were just matter, like what they say matter is and not how most matter really matters. what most matter does. which means every moment the parts of you part further from each other and then divide again. every moment more love beyond your reach. out. of your hands. so dangerous. and black.[2]

do listen. do love. do dance when the body feels heavy or blocked. we are always here. do trust that. do tell it to whoever is around in whatever way you can. do this. do this writing. do this writing like it is what it is. breathing. do breathe. do breathe while you can.[3]

speak loud and then hang up the phone. hang up the phone. hang up the phone. speak loud and then hang up the phone. i trust that you heard what i said.

quiet your mind and open your heart. open your heart.
    open your heart.
calm your mind down so you can open your heart.
    i'm not going to say it again.

dance well so you can leave it all there. leave it all there.
    leave it all there.
dance hard so you can leave it all there.
    soft with yourself and the pain.

wash clean so you can swim in your skin. shrug off the sin.
    be born again.
wash clean so the day can begin. i'm not going to say it again.[4]

so you listen to us all day every day. listen to us even more. so you love the folk always in every way. love the people even more. so you miss your father every day. miss him. miss him even more. so you promised her that you would stay. stay completely, feel it, be there, even more.[5]

it's your father

once the world opened and i found you. the you you could be, prop-ping the door like a stick of humanity. narrow version of yourself. the you you thought you had to be. daily, every minute. the world opened and i found you. the you you let through. the you that escaped despite you. the child you knew and allowed, once in a while, on summers and weekends. i found the you you were before everything. the you you were after everything. anyway. the you you couldn't stop being even when you wanted to or your parents begged.

another time the world opened and you had let go your structure your sticks your bones your legs and the world had opened your way out the way out you would leave me here.

once the world opened and i lost you. the you i thought i had and never had. the you i leaned on not knowing i had made you up my-self. the you i made myself by needing. the you you couldn't be but for so long. and now that you is gone, and the world is more than open, broken open, gaping. and i stand at the door screaming for the you you used to make for me for the you that held the space for me the you i let you take from me the you i made myself.[1]

you know how we do. tell the story over and over again at the table. laughing. knowing who among us will bellow. opening their voice to swallow all others. knowing who among us will swallow, pushing the below even further below. and the story becomes vivid. remembered by those who could never have been there. and some of us relive it. like we are shocked all over again. because the pain lives waiting for the chance to come out of the wings. i mean out of our lungs, which are becoming wings. i mean there was a way my father said *oh lord.* as punctuation and song when he was breathing. there was a way he witnessed and traveled when someone else was telling a story. there was a flex and bend in him become an instrument of memory. and what now. what now. i'm listening.[2]

i hated to see your skinned knees. the thick growing over. the magic work of blood. your skin rebecoming itself while you picked at it. i saw you perfect. in a first layer of skin. and you bit your nails, chewed the skin on your fingers, hazarded splinters like you didn't care. like you took it for granted. each layer of skin. you would stay in the sun and brown into brown like you strove for purple. you would keep neither hat nor glove on in heat or snow. you trusted your skin too much for my comfort. i saw you break yourself again and again. jumping from swingsets. dancing your hands out the window. roller-blades? why?

it must be the superhero TV shows you watch. what do you think you are made of? titanium? you are not. you are made of my love. you are made of the best of me in limited supply. because i am flawed. broken before you got here. guard your skin while you have it. shelter your bones. i should know. the good could run out.[3]

when we went, it was quiet with the neighbors whispering advice. soft with the sincere songs of children. hushed with shared and seasoned food. we went and Christmas was like sweetness sweat out the skin smiling. it was open doors and reasons to keep staying and keep talking. December in Anguilla was the wished-for reach of walking. it was Black love as it should be it was much too warm for stockings. it was time undone by listening and faith restrung by helping and the wealth was in the warmth was in the wellness was the hands the sand the sitting there the salt the smells the cooking days the songs remembered different ways the brown the bright the all of us. you never got to know that.[4]

i could hear you snore from down the hall. chainsaw to dreams, cutting them open, serrating them forever. so my dreams now all have edges, ridges, waves.

i could see you reading the newspaper in the bathroom, knees almost reaching the tub. open door barely clearing the toilet, but to me that bathroom seemed so big.

i could float on the waterbed that sometimes soaked the sheets. the plastic blue of break, the smart series of tubes, that seemed not smart at all to someone my age determined not to wet the bed. i knew that beds were for playing and that water could be anywhere.

i could smell the cinnamon, the sugar becoming air, the apples hot in their own juice, the lemon loving everything. the crust that we bought at the store and shaped to the pan like sculptors. i could smell it turning golden brown like us. and nothing said: *keep this. remember.*[5]

these things matter. what kind of apples you choose. how much cinnamon and sugar you use. how you shape the edge of the apple. how many you taste. how soon you add the lemon juice to protect from the browning of air. how long you bake the pie so the crust flowers brown like love. how clean the hands of daughters who want to help.[6]

supply and demand. the only black boy and the pressure of someone caring. the representative labor, the resentment. he calculates while he metabolizes lunch. he shares out his jokes while his classmates choke. he has been doing this math for a while. when one more black boy, not only black but also West Indian, joins the equation he is grateful. exponentially grateful. willing. abundantly willing to induct him into the quadratic. he will share the space he carved with wit and waiting. he shares it all and it becomes more. he will share his hard-earned lessons learned alone from all of the alone before. he multiplies time into as much time as possible with this bright new brother given by fate. he understands already that zero multiplied by anything is still zero. but still, if you add one to only it obliterates lonely. right? that's what he banks on. his shares of faith.

maybe if he had it to do again (he doesn't) he would calculate differently (now he can't) maybe he would have exchanged his welcome for a plot of escape or a warning rant. maybe there was something more necessary to learn than all that surviving and all that spite. certainly the intolerable stayed intolerable even when it was happening to both of them. right?

so two black boys and the eyes of small islands, the hands of striving fathers, the dying hands of legends. and all the smarts in the world and their stinging and their singing against the sharpest piece of air. and the years of decisions while they make all their choices and have all their children and lose all their hair. and their one prep school and their one university full of white boy legacy and dark shared knowing. and worlds of belonging turned longing and loss. universe of belonging turned longing and loss. and two black boys with each other at least. with each other at most.

and the cost.[7]

if you die angry what happens to the air. to the fires you didn't start but wanted to. if you die sad, the hot tears of early morning do they disrupt the cremation at all. if you die and there was something you wanted, but you couldn't make it happen, and you couldn't say it in a way that anyone could understand it. what then. what happens to the words. what happens to the poems, the screams, the sabbaths. what happens to the pauses you would have taken if anyone was listening. what about the sweat, the shake, vibration over phone lines and radio waves. what if you die unshaved. what happens to the pores unopened. and why doesn't death wait. when obviously there's something left to do.[8]

sand on a concrete floor. a painted concrete floor. sand painting its own whirlwinds on a blackened concrete floor.

put it on the menu.

this is the place of smoked chicken and understanding. of bright colors and reunions. of rebuilding something scraped along with chairs.

this is a place of inside made to look like outside. of strong wireless connections. of strong winds before and after barbed and circling wire.

where you came to be with your father. where i came to be with your father. where i came to be with you. where we came to celebrate you after.

the sound? it's a dub version of any top forty song over the last five years so a local reggae band can sing it sitting down. it's zouk playing out of bounds over St. Martin radio.

it's you. in Birkenstocks like your father used to wear. working all day and sleeping in your mother's old bed. it's you. shuffling side to side agile everywhere except the hips. it's you shaping sand with your shoes. painting your own black. it's you. now sand. in concrete.[9]

i put them in my two hands. a rock and a shell. or a piece of coral and a remnant of brick. or your face and my face and i try to wash them with tears. i try to clean them of everything i cannot say without crying again. i try to make them smoother and rounder than they can be. i hold them in my hands til they are glass. what happens to sand under the heat it takes for love to become loss? will it sear your skin first or slice it? what do i do but return to this water salted by your blood, your spit, your pee and snot and tears, your years as sun leached them out of you. what do i do with the wet of the debt of my still borrowed years given up. let the moon pull. let it write on the dark. it is not the same. the size of the sky. the glut of the ocean. your name.[10]

it got where being thirsty and wanting to cry were the same thing. salt-water irrepressible in your spirit. in your memory. in your membranes. you remembered thirsting before. you remembered before thirsting and couldn't reach it. you reached before memory. not all memory, but this particular memory. you thought you could cleanse it out by crying. you knew you couldn't. you thought if only i could cleanse it out by crying. or on the other hand deal with this salt. you thought if i could drink enough water. sweet water from fruit. filtered away from the mineral memories. if i could drink enough water. i could clean this wound forever. but the salt. you wake up and it's the salt. your whole chest a wound where everyone thinks blood is supposed to be. you realize everyone has already accepted this pain and you wake up feeling betrayed. and so thirsty you could cry.[11]

hard place of sidewalk shin splints. sharp place of saws cutting bone. get your tools away from my father. i said leave my father alone. harsh land of reluctant healthcare, bright maze of emergency rooms. if you cared anything about wellness, he wouldn't have left so soon. smooth place of lying answers, paper stacks of barrier walls. life doesn't have to be this heavy. shouldn't be this heavy at all. echo loop of media gunshots. replication of black on attack. my father does not belong to you. he's ours. now give him back.[12]

but what about the actual impact of weightlessness on the heart. the muscles. the bones. what happened to you. was it the result of all that space travel. and trying to come back. was it too much. too painful to be down to earth because your bones, because your muscles, because your heart. why have a body that needs the resistance of weight. why bear the gravity of this place anyway. why lay your burdens down in the first place if they were all that was keeping you here. or to paraphrase the hyperphysicists:

weightlessness is simply lack of support.[13]

white hole. that's what i want to call it now. the grief. evaporation of
the black hole. the last thing. when all the energy that was held, all
the light that could never escape, leaks out. in unpredictable ways.

is that the sound of outer space of reclaimed stars of supermassive
holes the size of many suns. the same sound i hear when it gets quiet.
like a child calling out. an angel screaming insistent. a longing. the
sound of a reaching that cannot stop. is that the sound that makes
the sky expand and everything get further apart like you from me
across the place i cannot go. like you from me. gone now with stars.
like you like you now love without air. like me from you with no way
back. the sound of me still needing you. the breaking sound. of my
bright black heart.[14]

even this cannot stay. this wailing grief. this opening void. even though this is not the last time, not the first time it has rent me thus. the sound in my brain of me screaming your name when everyone in the house is yet asleep and no one is disturbed but me. i move to the other side of it whether i want to or not. so who cares if i want to. i cannot keep this pain steady for the same reason i cannot reach you for the same reason i must therefore experience this breaking over and not over so over again.[15]

ribbons. i would use ribbons to tie you through to me, just retie carefully. looping silk. i would use grass, or palm fronds, braiding, indenting my hands. i would use twine if twine was what there was. i would use what there was to tie myself to you and get to where you are. i thought i had. i thought i already had.[16]

let's say life is stretched out in your muscles or woven inside your bones or tension in the tendons that keep you together. somewhere in that mix is something that is not flesh but life. let's say that. and that what happens might cause life's silken threads. (i imagine them as silver) to knot up, to contract. maybe to loop around as if they could make a spring of themselves to free you. but that freedom means a shorter and shorter life. and maybe that shorter life doesn't always look like years on the planet, but could look like time spent feeling joy. or purposeful presence or legacy. could life be all that, like the way you are remembered or not? if that was what life was, could i go in with fine-tooth comb and untangle, maybe use pliers where the wire is holding dear onto itself. icepick, chisel, bone saw? tell me what would i need to keep you longer. it can't be this. far distance between us. the stretching out of all my useless screams.[17]

whales are wise to stay far away. where they can pee in peace and process salt. they find each other by calling out. like i am calling you.

if the sound bounces back, between me and god, you are here. i can get the shape of you. if i were a whale would my kidneys be big enough, my gut a filter, could i drink these tears and swim forever.

they say our kidneys are small and relatively useless because we need all our energy to find food to eat. when did we start to hide food from each other. and our bodies. so cute. so physically naïve. did we think we wouldn't ever poison the water.

whales are wise. they stay far out at sea. if you chase in a boat they will spit in your face. in salt water, they call each other. like i am calling you.[18]

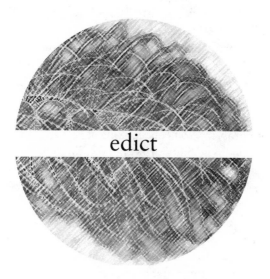

edict

you could say it was because we loved each other. because we wanted to live among each other. because we knew how to feed each other. we followed our relatives who had somehow learned to eat in this strange land. we were bunched up. and proud. and if you had asked any of us, we would have said we chose each other. preferred each other. and if we married people longer from this land we brought them too, close to what we claimed if not controlled.

someone looking at maps and measurements. someone owning and playing with property. someone looking at real estate as a game and not as the actual possibility of people you loved having somewhere to stay warm or not, might have come to a different conclusion. they would have no problem saying that we were there because no one wanted us elsewhere. we were there making them money too.

for me. i knew my own people. how to keep them warm. how to keep them cool and not just in body but in temperament. it was my people who paid for that car. the first car in Perth Amboy mind you. it was my people who paid for that truck i used to bring them coal in the winter, ice in the summertime. it was for our people out there playing cricket that my daughters would sell food and drinks. so it was also our people who paid their pocket money for school.

and for your grandmother, my daughter, it taught her something important about closeness. she never thought it was inconvenient to have all your cousins piled up with you like that. you could hear it in how she said all their names at once. in one breath. like they belonged together. no way she could have helped so many people if she didn't know close like she knew close. no way she could have managed those in between times that dreamers always have either.

that last time when you were with her, you your aunt and her all close again in that hotel room in Toronto. she was seeing more than the medication showed her. she was seeing me and more than me too. she was crowded again with the spirits who left but who never stopped calling her. and as much as she was always looking for somewhere to be, always wanting something new to see, she also never met a stranger in China or wherever she went. she was like you, already a cousin. already close. she was proud and unwilling to be trapped by anyone or anything, that's true. but ask her to name just one cousin. she will name at least three to start and she won't stop. ask her how many can fit, or who is welcome, or how far she can reach, or how much she can do and for how many. you'll see. she grew up American, but that crowded seeking space. that brought and bringing space. what would you say. the hold of the hold? she had it. and you. even you with all your training and time alone, you could well have it too.[1]

between their hands they passed his suits. they pressed the iron. they sharped his crease. the white the shirts they held them down they pulled the sleeves the heated folds. they took the work from mother. begrudged it of each other. the work that never stopped. they shopped. they cooked. they overlooked. they pressed the weekly wear. they left and stayed and felt betrayed behind the shape of clothing made. the pants the slants the waiting stance the never-questioned shape. the deepest black the heart attack the man he thought he was. the weekly baking. daily taking. crazy making love. three daughters. two wives. with stolen lives and unacknowledged beauty. he killed them all, before the fall. with the privilege of their duty.[2]

they fell? to me it didn't feel so innocent. they were clawed and taken. the question being only, by whom? by god? by my own greed? in exchange for cars or clothing? what was bought if they were price? what could make it happen twice? three times? it was worse the longer it took, the closer look i got. it was not at all helpful to hear that i would see them in heaven like angels. i was like any African woman deprived of sons. i was ashamed. i was rageful. i could see them right here where i was. in hell.[3]

have you seen it. you have seen it. a woman out of range. no longer swallowing her rage. raw in the throat. you have seen it.

with me it was *never tell me anything again.* you can't. you can't ever tell me anything again. it was the first contract broken. it was the core of the earth screaming. a mother's intuition is not surface or convenience. a mother's intuition is from the core of the earth. that much heat. *i said don't touch me. don't tell me any telling, stuff your sayings about soon or another son. i will burn you. i am burning with what i know and what i knew. don't you ever touch me.*

that's why he sent me here. because there was nothing he could tell me. and really he could look at me and know. there is no authority after this. i am the author of my child's life. you cannot tell me. and that means i am responsible for his death. *you will meet me in this hell or leave me alone. my child is mine. i hear him screaming. i hear him calling me. i don't hear you.* i can't hear anything but screams. who is that calling out? i gave my baby to the devil. *no i can't come back. you sold my baby you proud devil in your creased black suit. hid him to suit you. my love is mine. and now it burns too wild to hear you. leave me here. i am never coming home.*[4]

on the walls she could see everything. she did not have to scratch the designs with her nails. maybe she did it. but she didn't have to. visually. what work she made of walls was because she could not stop her hands from moving. most of the time. she could not stop her blood from flowing. until she could. she used her nails and her need. she shaped it herself. tomb for a woman without sons.

womb for a woman without words. worse was the silence. and more necessary. she could see stars but could not hear her daughters. she could hear the sharp voices of aunts saying "wait." she could want the clumsiness and dirt of boys but could not keep it. could never arrive at a smaller version of her large husband again. easier to control and truly hers. through the hearse she heard the hollow cries of all those watching. no longer jealous. calling her the heathen that she was.

some days she made a choir in there by herself. and the attendants were too tired to distinguish it from screaming. some days she let the aunts sing loud, let the old ones drum. some days she danced in there and made stars with her hands. and placed them like components of a crown around her head. but soon it got too heavy and if there was any point. if there was anything sharp enough to get her out of this joint. it would have to go through her skin.

jesus. the place she was in. could have been heaven. could have been a monastery or retreat. needed to be artful days and ways to work through grief. but it was not any of these. it was the madhouse where the women artists went to wail their waste. it was the center of the universe. her place.[5]

i thought at least in my house. i thought at least in my house i could make everything right. i could make everything clean. i could make everything bright. at least in my house. but even in my house there was night. and at night i had dreams and at night i couldn't scream because it would wake the children up. so i saved the shards in my throat and they became the edge i used all day to get those same children to clean up and pick up and sit up and stop and obey. because i had this daydream that in my own house i could make everything okay. and for me that was linked to looking a certain way.

i wouldn't say artist. i wouldn't say that. i would say someone who sees. and i didn't know until you told me that the people who see *are* the people who clean. and the reflectiveness of the surfaces can be so seductive and be so mean because i don't want to see all this. and if shining the silver means you will see chains you have to do something to protect your brain. so make the kids do it. and if wiping the mirror shows you the hell of all your people and you don't know the spell then yell about fingerprints. and if your fingers tap out codes that belong in elegiac odes what can you do about that. but snap and point and chide and holler and play the piano to try to swallow what the hymns are showing you. and when the kids keep growing you know even their faces bear traces that ghosts have been showing you too. no one knows what you're going through.

i mean no one knows what i'm going to do. and that's why the place is jumpy and quiet and shaking but still. that's why my husband is afraid of the breadth of my will. and why even though i married the coal man my house has a chill. and it is not okay. and i couldn't stay. so they sent me away.

play the songs with the blues women howling. play the gospel of voices that crack. play the stories and clean the whole house up. scream your truth and invite me on back. let the mirrors be oceans and swim them. let the silver be unlock and key. tell the children you love them and need them. set me free.[6]

edgegrove

if you hadn't asked. if you hadn't been there during cards. if you had not unlearned your fear of the sudden slam of dominoes. if you hadn't wondered. if you hadn't trusted. if you hadn't come home from school on weekends. if you hadn't loved the folk. if you hadn't loved the people West Indian and winded and stranded in Perth Amboy. if you hadn't loved too recklessly and had to leave home. if you hadn't outgrown the island and thought yourself the world. if you hadn't wanted to see, to know, to make. if you hadn't been so consistently nice. if you hadn't been so afraid of becoming your mother. if you hadn't been so afraid of becoming your father. if you hadn't lived through nightmares and found back the day. if you hadn't watched their hands until you learned how to play. if you hadn't felt so at home and wanted to stay. if you hadn't needed. if you hadn't joked. if you hadn't made the uniform into a platform instead of a yoke. if you hadn't walked both ways to high school and home. if you hadn't sounded white enough over the phone. if you hadn't took what you got and traded it for stone and coal and ice. if you hadn't been so nice that the whole neighborhood knew about it and called up your name as advice. if you hadn't stayed despite the rumors. if you hadn't had an iron sense of humor. if you hadn't fed them and named them and claimed at least some of them. if you hadn't played. if you hadn't listened like life depended on it. listened like people who knew shells. listened like salt that survived water. listened like you'd been through hell. i wouldn't be able to hear you so well.

so thank you.[1]

he said:

in my time it was more of a practical decision. you knew what you needed. you knew what you didn't know how to do. you knew what you didn't want to learn. you knew having a wife had an impact on what you could earn. you knew having children and keeping them around was the only thing that could dampen the sound of your own screaming for your father. at your father.

so you needed someone who could do it. who would stay and work and make and take from you what you needed to be big enough to give. there was love, but it was not a decision made from flutters or good feelings. it was mostly a decision to live.

she said:

for me, it wasn't a given, but it meant something. my younger sisters didn't do it. many aunts never, my own daughter. i couldn't place my value on the ability to have sons. that was what my mother had done. and it didn't work. but also, in his face, i saw a faraway place. that he guarded with oceans and eyelashes. and what do i do, when i see a limit, but go. i could not know. and not knowing has been my refrain, my motivation and my bane. the air i breathe. so even though i may have been as romantic as anyone else. i knew my father wanted a reproduction of himself. and didn't have it. and when the chance came, though i didn't look eager, i grabbed it. believe what you want to believe.

it was mostly a decision to leave.[2]

you could make paper dolls that looked like us. brown with well-defined lines. bright clean clothes. generations of cultivated listening for when to smile, when to pause, when to say something, make you laugh. you could fold skirts around our waists and tools into our hands. spatulas, and books, pens and knives. you can sense the perforation in our lives. push and separate us from the scene. sturdy enough to stand, thin enough to bend, this is what i mean:

here is the mother. she smiles and smiles. her hair is round around itself and smooth. here are her skirts. her aprons. shoes. sheet music, cookie sheet, hospital corners. sewing machine included.

here is the father. unending laugh. he is already bald. his head. it shines. here are his hands. they can hold anything. the sun, large stones, and other burdens.

here is the girl. her head tilts east. she sees something. what does she see. her hand is outstretched. one hand raised and open. the other one pats a cute little dog.

there is the boy. both feet on the ground. is his hand in a fist or is he holding a truck. his mouth is open as if in speech. what will he say. too much.[3]

mother and daughter sit at the piano. mother sits. daughter stands. daughter sings over mother's shoulder. doesn't know what to do with her hands. mother sounds the keys like warnings. mother throws her voice like rope. daughter reads the sacred words. daughter holds the holding notes. mother bangs like god is coming. mother shouts the angels down. daughter shapes her lungs to bellows. daughter gives her heart to sound. mother makes the marks the meaning. mother means the mothers march. mother masks the pain of cleaning. breathing wrinkles back the starch. daughter draws the door on dancing. daughter dares the day to stay. mother stills the shaking hands of her own mother every time she plays. daughter dreams the darkened many. daughter dreams the curtain calls. mother makes the time stop moving. mother makes the heavens fall. daughter doesn't see the window. daughter only sees the sun. daughter sings the stalwart alto. mother hears it when she's done. daughter mother daughter mother daughter mother song become.[4]

clean lined notebook pages and the possibility of a right answer. at
some point even graph paper and lead. the tried predictability of
numbers. the careful study of the whitened dead. the uniforms, per-
mission slips and pennies. the lunches and the creases and the shine.
the possibility that there won't be any humiliating childhood affronts
this time. the sandwiches the shopping and the showing. the stern
reviews of all returned reports. the singing and debate team and the
growing. the service and the showmanship and sports. the stinging
and the struggling and chafing. the only and the ownership and owe.
the learning living right beside forgetting. the things they leave be-
hind them when they go. the way they come back people we don't
know.[5]

we told them time was fine, but you needed money for when the world would fall out under you. we said the world will fall out under you. we said take care of your family because family is all you have you know, the world will fall out under you. but we didn't necessarily say trust them. we said be the rich relation not the one seeking crust of bread and such. we did not say shame but you saw it. we said work hard but we didn't say you can change the world. we said the world is the world. learn it but don't trust it. become it but don't trust it. and so you cannot trust each other. we see that now.[6]

she sent them with sharp sewn clothes out of the latest patterns. she sent them with lines and creases to memorize. she sent them with prayers sewn in by her dancing fingertips. she sent them blessed by her needle-biting mouth.

she had sewn her graduation dress. did you know that? well they had all sewn their graduation dresses, but hers won the prize. and she went across small water to Pratt Institute. and scrubbed toilets to sit next to people who didn't want to touch her hand. who denied the magic in her hems. her everything small knots. what her elegant seams.

and she knew how to design other things too. like dollhouses and life. like like and love. like women's organizations and performance gloves. like sponge puppets and meals. and events and hair. and a face that could face the unending stares.

she clothed them to prepare them for the office of only. so at least they wouldn't be cold since they probably would be lonely. she sewed *so what* out of silk, organdy, and tweed. she sewed pockets into trust and pleats into need. she sewed sweat and forget into linings like seeds. she dressed them well. for school.

and as far as you could tell. school wasn't hell. she went back herself when she could. and said despite what those people said or did, school was inherently good. and if you lose focus you should . . . you should not lose focus because you are the great nieces and nephews of proud black teachers who could. not. stop. even. if. they wanted to. they got dressed and went another day. and you are dressed in that debt anyway. stitch your eyes to the prize girl. stay.[7]

he is small and brown. he is the last of nine. he cannot see the words in their heads, but he can see the clothes that differentiate. he is wearing a sack. a flour sack. his mother had used the flour to make bread for the workers who pass by. the salt of her sweat and the thread makes it something else. he is clothed in the breakfast of back-breaking labor. he is just barely not naked. enough to sit here in school. and in school the children are sick and are sneezing and the tall white teacher hates the heat and the brown. and the tall white teacher was sent here for spite. and the tall white teacher sees only his own failure. and the tall white teacher cannot quiet his mind. so he beats the children saying *be quiet be quiet*. he beats them with leather for a cough or a sneeze.

and where can he go. this small boy who cannot make his body not sneeze. who cannot make his body less loud than the teacher's outrage. who has barely anything to wear, let alone something to wipe his face. where can he go except the darkness of forgetting. the practice of remembering the letters etched in night. where can he go except the poems he remembers, cram them into hungry places where he must push out the light. the almost naked child claims the one place the tall white teacher cannot touch. and shapes it into a hiding place he will give to generations. it is sharp with the edges of slate written letters. it is tangled with the cursive of cursed colonized children. it is a choking place where we go to breathe.

go to school.

so it is not a surprise that he sent his children to places where they would have to eventually use the retreat. where their bodies were not safe and their hearts were not wanted and their minds would become weapons. would be sharp as any machete. would cut and decipher with wit more than wisdom. he clothed them in his fine spun survival. they added pockets and pouches for the other ways they would be hurt. the nicknames. the teasing. the ignorance. the games. the stacked up rejections. the sitting there. the shame. they would escape into the work itself and come out the best. with paper as refuge. because it wasn't the real test.

but a child cannot distinguish. a grandchild even less between the tall white teacher and herself at her best. between pain itself as spiritual teacher, and the suffering tantrum of white educational space. she has learned to quiet her heart. she has learned to fix her face. but she notices that when life gets hard, when grief is trying to teach. just then just then, she retreats. to what? to school. to tasks. to questions she has been asked that she thinks she can answer. specifically? to email.

what's the matter with school? you leave and go there. you go there and leave. and leave some more. but she is learning. slowly learning. how to stay.[8]

unlearning herself

first i will fall into myself. breathing my own heart beyond my back. into the black beneath the floor i lie upon.

first i will fall back. my black heart breathing beyond the lie i tell into myself.

first i will black my heart. breathing my own beneath. myself. my floor. my lie. my fall. beyond that.

in fall i will breathe first. the heart of the lie. myself. the floor of my back. beyond.

i will lie beneath black. beyond breathing. my heart. myself. upon falling. first.[1]

first i thought i was my thoughts. that's what i was thinking. i thought i was making myself with my brain through understanding more and more of myself. understanding you as myself. understanding everything under me as myself everything over me as my standing. underneath that, i was scared to death. because i knew that i didn't know nothing.[2]

before i knew how to say it, i knew. before i knew that you knew too, i knew. before i heard anyone else say it was true, i knew. but that doesn't mean i can't know something else. you know?[3]

she learned about the thousand paper cranes and couldn't fold even one. she was confused about the cure for cancer and papercuts and the differential static electricity of hers and other people's hair. she had heard some but not enough about flyaway. she was wary of balloons. she was not patient enough to braid a proper friendship bracelet (or a proper friendship either, she would find out later). there were children's books about radiation and a constant state of war. there was elementary school itself, a daily battle. she had a backpack that weighed almost as much as she did. she had a Swiss Army knife she wanted to show her friends. she had a subpar sticker collection and a far above average reading level. they put her name on a plaque, they made her Phillis Wheatley in the play. she had no peers.[4]

sometimes when she walked along the street with someone holding her hand she would look for rainbows in the gutters made of oil. and in the asphalt parking lot spots where leaking cars had been. it was the best representation of her beliefs. that and the planetarium she had seen once. she would go home and try to draw dark rainbows using every crayon color until the paper became wax thick breakthrough dark and layered like the universe and none of her crayons could ever call themselves clean. or flesh colored. or burnt. again. she didn't know at the time that not every child had access to all the crayons they could want and bleachered boxes with their own sharpener in the back. because all the children at her school had even more crayons and markers and stickers and the matching skin that looked like what the box said skin was and this cute way of drawing the lines thicker with color and then gently shading it in. that was not her way.

in those days she would not have said it was her critique against the flat white post-Columbian world. she would not have said she was drawing a map to the thick starred place where she came from. she would also not have said it was an abstraction. because though the blobs of intersecting colors, purple until it was not purple any more, deeper like the many angles of love, did not make a known shape, a discrete angle or anything that could be called a figure, there was a satisfaction she felt when she knew she had done it. there. which meant it was something she could recognize. and it was representation for her already long fingered hands. it was at least a response to not being represented in the box and the sweet elementary curriculum. did anyone keep those drawings? probably not. but if you found one, you could use it to read everything she does now. her whole approach really. all the colors. all the colors pushing hard against white paper with the core creative craving for it. black.[5]

she had quiz cards bolted to each other with plastic, in fanned-out divination. she ate color-coded reading-level assessments like candy until they ran out. she knew what they wanted you to know. she knew the counterintuitive shapes they made again and again with their testing and telling. she knew what white people were saying far away without seeing their (hard-to-see) lips. she had been sent in at the age of two so she would know. like the woman on the TV show who learned to assemble and disassemble weapons as a child to one day be herself a weapon the end of children the perfect spy. but this was real life in the unreal. she knew this system by instinct. could tell you what was missing in any complex sentence. could show you what was hidden behind any choice of tense. could explain to you all of television with the thing on mute. to some people it seemed like she could read minds. it was easy.

it was necessary. because you may not hear them coming. they might be out of sight. they do not speak a truth-telling language. they will lie on purpose and forget they are lying. they will train themselves not to know in the first place. and nothing has to be announced, nor written down anywhere. you know that. you don't have to know, though you usually do, what they think they are saying and why. you don't have to know, though it's obvious now, what they do to the children and the sky. and you noticed already, that what they do to water they will do their mothers and you.

you cannot not know what it means. and we trust you to know what to do.[6]

first. she gave away all her books. no. that wasn't really the first thing. that took a lot.

first she took care to memorize the names she heard as prayer and to pray them back. three times at least. then she started to trust herself to remember what she had learned from all the books, the reading of them and the writing of them. she had to trust the things that were not books and were not made by people. she had to trust the things that were not things but god itself growing on earth. earth itself as rock and information. she had to trust those things which were only as real as she was to prompt her memory or her knowing or more than that. her pulse. her impulse to come out and make sound or movement. and she had to trust that those sounds and those movements could be enough for whoever was out there. and that she could live with it forgive with it if they said *no. it isn't enough.* because how could she know the prayers of other people? how could she measure the listening of other people how could she gauge the trust of other people when she was learning still learning to trust herself and move. in the trust she found out there were no other people. no out. she found in. and behold to let go. everything was there. and it was then that she gave it all away. no matter how it looks. and the first things she gave up were all of those books.[7]

some of the one million times that wrong was my name.

when the white girls at school thought they were saying it and they weren't saying it. when you called and i saw and i wasn't doing anything and i still didn't pick up the phone. when i built a life specifically out of decisions designed to keep you from saying, she isn't doing anything, and used that life of decisions i made to avoid the lot of you. when i said i couldn't, which is always a lie. when i didn't say what i didn't want because i thought silence would be better. when i trusted silence to protect me even though Audre Lorde had already said. when i typed an email instead of shouting and didn't capitalize nothing but the grammatically required. when my sister used on me the look my mother used on us and closed the door. when i told them i was from New York because i didn't think anyone had ever heard of New Jersey. when i told them i was from somewhere with one name. when i let the limits of their understanding be the limits of my communication because i just didn't want to be bothered. when i wasn't bothered by all the things, all the things. when i pretended to be concerned but was just bored and ready for you (whoever you are) to get to your next feeling, or grow or something. when i assumed you already knew. when i thought i could punish you by being so stellarly visibly amazing in your face. when i decided you weren't worthy of the time it takes to ask. when i hoarded all my words for the poems and said the people, well, the people will be okay. when i spelled it (this is my name we are talking about) with letters only left by empires only spellable in blood. when i fixated on how my baby brother said mud, but didn't call the young man he became as much as i could have called. when i stalled on asking for anything because of how scared i was to know the no you had waiting for me and why. when i thought i wouldn't die so i could just do it later.[8]

what if you could float? what if you stretched your legs and the air held them as easily as water. the dust held them as easily as salt. would you stop working then? would you trust me then? would you let go then? or would you still run off, lustful as you are for ground to bury yourself in again?[9]

yes of course. it is always about the mother. it is not ever not about the mother. worlds of rage. there is always something screaming for the mother. this is why we rarely act our age. mother is a six-letter word holding far too much longing and far too much grief. mother is half a word. what did you call me? come here. you thief.[10]

even after you stop running from the truth, the truth can still escape you. or that's what truth is. your sweat made vapor. your light unreadable. your love uncaught. your labor unbought. for now.[11]

what if i told you i made the shape of your world with my hands. poured enough water onto dirt and oil to knead and reknead it. introduced land to itself again. what would you say?

and if i said your first fears in the morning, loudest cries in your sleep, sweetest solace, i made those too. added them in like spices and fruit and built you back around them like so much dough. what would you do?

and if i said i could make you from anything, replace or add anything, roll you out any thickness, cut your edges any curve, then what? what would you ask for?[12]

it wasn't so much that she could predict the future. it was more that she could breathe into the past. open her body to the forgotten. re-live it other ways. she could do it any day as if no one had ever died. or since dead as if no one had been lost. or since lost as if the lessons lasted like love or what would have been love, if someone had been waiting with an impossibly open heart. if someone had been still enough to still sense it anyway. yes. sense. so she made that her work.[13]

birth chorus

if you spread us out like pictures on a line. or better if you try to spread us out, like paper dolls of yourself, folded along the edge of generations. you will have a problem. *how does it feel?* you will not find a middle. a normal. a self to keep being. if that is what you are looking for. *is it?* put us on this paper, page after page so you can see us, facing morning so we can see you, you will be surrounded and astounded. you will be surprised and thoroughly revised. you will not be the you you thought you knew.[1]

we are the ones who were never born. who were born and lost. who were lessons unready for learning outside. crucial for learning inside.

we are the ones made of lining and longing and spilled. dirt and hurt tilled for what was done and not quite over.

we are the names chosen and put away. or given to others. we are the ones who did not stay. but then we do. we are the nails and edges of you. we are the waiting and wonder of you in the womb. we share a wide tomb, dug for small boxes, like shedding foxes, hair and red. we are the actual undead, too real for movies. we are the knowing and growing and small. we are the accumulated unenumerated squall. we are the rungs that punctuate the fall. we exist in a way you didn't know how to call. forth. until now. that's all.[2]

some of us did have names. and were wanted and were dreamt about and were spoken to. some of us do have names, but they're very rarely spoken now. for a while they were always soaked with tears. slowly the sounds that used to call us float apart between each other. the resolve to remember dissolves over the years. like what would have been our bones.

all of us did have names. and were known before we became strangers. all of us did have names that were spoken long after we were taken. but who would name their child after one who was stolen. who would let their presence steal away the loss. who would write over our prayers with their forgetting and at what cost. we all had names and our surviving would not keep them. not for long enough to give and make again. our names. sometimes we treasured them like breathing. sometimes we spat them out, unanswered prayers.[3]

we made the planet round so we could hold you. made that one star bright enough and pulled you close. we are still shaping this planet, like a baby's head. are you symbiont or parasite. playmate or pest. we made this planet round, surrounded on all sides by sound, surrounded in all spaces by us. we can as easily cradle you as crush.[4]

we withhold work when we want. when we want you to wait. when the weight needs to pull you into dreams in the day. pull your time into stopping and looking or dropping and rolling. come wallow with us. work is for the weak. tarrying is for the brave. dallying is for the descendants. work is for the slave. work ignores the grave. work would stave away the words we want to say, so we withhold work. we want water and worn clothes and what you should have done before. sometimes we wait. and stack sadnesses ignored and heartbreak hoarded and we take you out for a whole day. without warning. we slug into your morning. reclaim it for mourning. usually on a deadline when something is due. everything is owed. the something is you. when we want you we'll waste your whole day.[5]

we see you. with your lightweight machines and swift work. we see your large kitchen empty of smoke. your soft hands and unstung eyes. we don't know why you would trust to eat food shipped from thousands of miles or anything wrapped in plastic when it reaches you though we do note how it lessens the squatting and the reaching and the burn and the dirt and the bites and the all day long of what we did. but what about the lessons and the muscles and the teaching and the learn and the worth and the rites. and how long we lived without your air-conditioned prison healthcare, without your unsweated natural hair. we see you and recognize some of our short-lived wishes that we didn't have much time to wish because of work to do. we see the convenience and are often amazed, but not, at the end of it, impressed.[6]

most of the time we were making it with our hands. that which you call life and buy in boxes over increments. we were patting each other's knees and shoulders. making life. that which you siphon down to half-spelled words and cartooned texts. we were calling it up with our throats. those prayers that you garble into screen names. not you in particular, daughter. you in general.

and that's the thing. we didn't have time to be so particular. we just wanted life in general. and one person couldn't have it and keep it. if any of us were to have it, we would all have to share what we had and make more. that's what they mean, the old ones, when they call you spoiled. even though they are the ones that spoiled you. you want to forget that life doesn't keep. life doesn't store. not in this heat for sure. that's what i'm telling you. share life today. and then make fresh life for tomorrow.[7]

our children belong to us. you belong to us. the world we making. though we may not have each time intended you. you were ours from the breaking, not theirs for the taking. we fought for that. and the scream around our belonging is our own long longing to be held. and how it hurts to be fought for with just a few small tools while the whole world destroys us. our children do not belong to the men who made them upon us. we do not keep their names. we do not keep their names close. you will remember us by our first names. the names our mothers called us. our children belong to us though we cannot protect them. we are not speaking of your safety. just an illegal claim. we are saying your name. you belong to us.[8]

teeth. we paid. usually in teeth and dreams. teeth and dreams and calories, mostly iron. stomach lining and the lining of clothes that wore out where no one could see. patches of hair we thought we could afford and edges of nails reddened by worry.

we paid for loving you with days and nights of openness. anytime being punchable in the gut. all the ways they could hurt us through you. we paid with renewable grief and one hundred thousand different fears. we paid with all our credit. all our credibility. because we cared too much. because we loved you, they could always say we were over-reacting. they could always say we were biased. we paid with never being neutral again. never again capable of hiding where we stood. we stood with you. which meant we could not be clean. which meant we could not be taken anywhere without making a scene. the same scene over and over again upon separation. our time turned into a recurrent dream. our bodies never again whole. our minds full and so often leaking. you. we paid for loving you with you yourselves. each changing self. the losing you we feared and underwent over and over again like once wasn't enough to make us long forever. once there was you, once any of you, then all time became loss. every moment holding mourning, always knowing what we could not keep which was you. ourselves. or anything. it was everything. literally everything. the price we paid for loving you.[9]

what they took? what they took. was touch. what they took. was taste. every touch become iron. every taste become deficiency. every day become craving. what they took. was sight. meaning what you saw would have to be known by the way they unsaw you. what they wanted was everything. every tooth every skin cell every muscle every vocal chord every hand that could still drum. what they wanted was to live forever. what they wanted was to outrun death. so they chased us like the unchaste after lust.

and retake the stakes. unshake the breaks. make out the fake open the ache taste back our touch we must.[10]

we didn't have so much of what you call corsets. or access to ribbons and eyelets and gowns. under their gowns what they wanted was a shape like ours. so what we had was breathing. you can breathe into any muscle, you know. any muscle. no matter how small or how tired. no matter how overused or bruised. sometimes you had to small your breathing so nobody could see what you were doing. sometimes that illusion of small was what you were making with a breathing that went up into your head instead of down into your belly. sometimes the suggestion of slightness in the face of whiteness was all that saved your life. because they would have killed you if they could see, blamed you for the seeing of themselves. so you sent breath exactly where it was needed like an economist under sanctions. you willed yourself the tentative boundaries of your pores, you made them quiet in some places, a low vibration so no one would hear because unnoticed was unharmed.

or sometimes you made the sweat sweet air around your skin shake loud and loose because being unnoticed was in fact the fastest way to be harmed. you could only trust yourself about when and where. and that was how you got to know god. you learned to listen to the un-hearable. you learned to check for the smallest things. because how small were you yourself. and it resonated with you that god would kill his best most loving child, because though you paid attention to every sign it didn't always work. and when it didn't work, the intel-ligent breathing, the hiding in plain sight, you lost everything, your children and your chest and the boundary of light around your skin. you lost your chin, your kin, and your sleep. and you had no breath-ing left to weep, you had used it all.

and by you, of course, we mean us. you are not small at all, except for what we taught you. except for what our breathing took and what it bought you. you are not small even slightly. we are telling you this for the depth of what you might be. you are not small unless your own breath-ing shrinks you. and you need not do that now. don't take it lightly.[11]

first we tried it with sweat. and then everything else. until we were too dehydrated to secrete. so then we took our secrets, dried the salt and emptied those onto each other blunt with silence. and then we asked for each other's blood with teeth. we took metal and went in to try to find it. took syringes and tried to replace it. we tried everything.

in the end there was no sand that could scrub us clean. no paper, green or otherwise, that could absolve us. there were only gods who told us stories in the language of our losing. there were potions that made oceans rise in our guts. there were tears if we were lucky, but mostly the opposite of tears. there were screams if we were blessed, but mostly the opposite of screams stabbing our organ linings. there were medical terms for where we kept everything we could not let go. everything that should never have been ours in the first place. you know?

but imagine someone taking you and flaying you and making your skin into death and death again and remaking your body and saying they are doing it because god. and then all you have left is your flesh. and you got to take the god out. because they said what they said and did what they did. they said god. and you try everyday to unpray the inevitable. to spell out the spell backwards. but you cannot extract god from flesh. you cannot though you try. so every day you know better. but it still hurts.[12]

there was a series of us. who saw what creative power could and could not do and what could happen when you gave it over to men. we couldn't stomach it. not men and their pageantry. that we often enjoyed. but the theft. like how they hand the baby over to the father as if the mother was the most simple of errand girls delivering a squalling message about their manhood. and tip for the messenger. annual flowers for the messenger. it made us sick.

we might not have said it out loud but we kept all the things we noticed in tightening jewelry bags fastened by ribbons in our heads. the beveled edges in our torsos. fortified boxes in our hearts. with keys we gave only to other people's children who mostly didn't understand the concept of anything being locked away at all. which is why we loved them. which is not to say trusted. we saw how under certain circumstances, rather normal circumstances, what you make is trained to betray you, forget you, and let you go mad. we saw it happen again and again. so we decided.

we would make things that could only bear our names or none. sometimes we would make new names to bear them. sometimes we would kill them in our minds. more often we would give it away to everyone, what we could make. or make it so quietly in such a daily way that it became part of something stronger then the men we knew. the breathing that holds the bricks together in black churches, libraries, and schools. you have felt it? that was us. we trained ourselves to turn our words to fertile dirt unceded to plow. we discovered how to bake our dreams in summer sun to insulate the cold that chased our bones. we chose to live our lives alone or in the company of nieces and each other. we slept with other people's husbands in the middle of the week, or we rebuffed them. we ate extravagant meals and then forgot them. we were lifetime members of the NAACP and AME. we bought so many beautiful things we couldn't keep. we passed the stories on like helix lines and blood. we told them to ourselves to go to sleep.[13]

what do we believe in? the local power of the sun. the way light, once activated, secondhanded as it may be through plant and animal and mother, must be honored. must be honored as much as the sun itself. you cannot honor only a piece of the sun. one angle of the sun. one ray of light at a time. you look ridiculous trying to love just some people. just some animals. just some plants some of the time. you don't love some. you love all. or you don't at all. that's what we learned.

what do we know? the staying power of the dark. how whatever you do there is still more you cannot, do not know. the future is black. you don't even know half the past or what is happening now. which is why they can't kill us how they want to. even if all they do all day is try. which is why they are afraid. which is why we are afraid. which is why you are afraid, wondering if you we or them.

the black thing is that we this them don't break down don't make no sense in the dark where you can't see yourself and say you know. the black thing is you all the nothing.

you can't see someone else and say you already know. and they don't know either. all that possibility. all that disconnect between seen and unseen. unseen always outnumbering like dark matter in the sky. all of us down here where you can't do nothing but dirt. like a seed. dark with maybe. you we they all grow.[14]

if you could see it. turn it horizontal and look. you would see. the decisions stacked like tiny pieces of paper. millimeters of coral. milligrams of plaque in the arteries. undeniable indentations in the frontal lobe or heart. if you could see it. we can see it, but you can't see it from there. what you can see is what happened to us. what you can see is what still don't happen. what you can see is actually enough. take the scale of a day. take the scale of the life of a live person a different age from you. take the sister scale of compassionate consideration across. take it as communication from us. or take us as communication from the source. i mean trust it. it adds up to all of what we do. subtracts and multiplies the same way. divides you from you and us from you and all of us is that and them. and trust also this. you the we. the this beyond this. the form and the function the content and the coefficient. and any of that can change (you. us.) and when it changes, let it change everything.[15]

some days we held in the sky for you. colored it with colors you would recognize. primary. it was clear where one color ended and another one started, we sewed them together with your future. things you would one day know for yourself. and if you followed the lines they would lead to an opening, a circle way through to the other larger sky with all its inconstancy and trouble, but in the world of colors, smooth fabric stretched by air, held by hands in a circle, hands belonging to people who knew what to do because of the words of a poem they had taught themselves just then, you felt so safe. and it was only for a few seconds, soon it would be your turn to go back out into the regular unregulated sky and take your own turn holding the fabric and answering the poem, but during those few seconds you imagined you could live in there forever and be free. remember that.[16]

conditions

the is the song of starving children. this is the song that silence sings. these are the singing bones of babies. these are ribcages shaped like wings. these are the sounds of souls distending. season salt of mothers' tears. this is the song of no good reason, the failure of love for a thousand years. this is the song of boats and bellies. this is the song of burning brains. this is the song of bruising and blisters and emptied shells on echoed days. this is the cost of freedom's pretense. this is the taste of glut and waste. this is the song we make by placing fear into compassion's place. this is the song we wake up singing. written in sharps and never flat. this is the song of starving children. the world we know is made of this.[1]

some people talk about infectious disease. the germs brought by the cold people from the cold places after months of eating nothing but meal and then they let their germs eat us alive and called us cannibals. the lies. the lies they tell on us.

but what if there is a form of infection more insidious and reproducible across generations. the form being the form itself. the form being the thing that brought them and made them bring us, the other us, is the same us, before the form or because of the form. form meaning the form of life that would register as life from then on. it would manifest in several ways. water in the mouth. lust over the possibility of a suit. a seemingly harmless question about whether you own a house. or decades of resentment over whether someone made something of themselves as if selves were made by selves themselves and designed to be improved upon like shelves of goods. as if by this manner we would sell ourselves and always come up short. and then hate each other for it. as if we didn't need each other more than that. as if we got here not of body but initially of boat. as if every lie were true that they used on me and you. in other words as if there was no such thing as life or love at all.[2]

this is the problem with owning. it gets into your blood. it replaces your blood with something like a self-justifying story. the story circulates from your heart out to your hands, from your heart up to your brain. oh no. in fact that's not it. the story circulates from your brain to your hands. from your brain out of your mouth. the heart is cut out of the deal. and the story does not keep you warm. it is thinner than blood if only slightly younger. it can belong to you and distract from other longings. unlike blood it only binds you to one life. the life you think they gave you. the life you made yourself.

in the story, when god had a body he used it to build things. he used it to show the possible. then he let it bleed out. blood was what he shared at the table. or actually wine, again and again instead of blood, instead of water. take this cup from me he said, like Moana in the Disney movie. choose someone else. the thing is there is no one else, to look after, to be. there is no one left to thank you.[3]

the trees knew. the trees and the ferns and the moss and the lichen knew. the rocks knew and seemed to do nothing about it. the bacteria in your eyes, between your teeth, roaming the smooth expanse of your stomach knew and acted. the bats knew with their sensitivity to shape. the mosquitoes knew, full as they were with the blood of captured and capturing alike. the sharks knew already underwater. the whales sang of what it would mean. and the smallest plankton had to get ready after centuries of making life out of sun. the coral had to get ready after perfecting collaboration bright solid and grown. the birds and the fish must have known the implications. once a species could do that to itself. do this to itself. what we do. get ready for the influx of carbon dioxide, the mountainous islands of trash. the unearned permanence of plastic. all life would have to change the meaning of breathing. they all knew.[4]

Jamaica

sunrise. full moon. heat. they turned their hearts towards the east for other reasons. more than just opposition. and it didn't take Garvey to tell them. it didn't take a mystic to understand why having your back to the treacherous west took practice and bravery. how not falling apart every day was meditation. or how else did they show up clean and smiling after their dignity was boot-trampled on the hour. they turned. they turned their hearts. towards heat. full moon. sunrise.[1]

would you say they thought of themselves as black or would you say they thought of themselves as light-skinned relative to somebody. would they have explained their irrational admiration of the burning skinned the pale white soldiers who stayed, skin reddened by sun and mosquito bite. would you say it was convenience or striving that had them name everything hot they drank "tea," when really it was made from cocoa or bush i mean whatever they actually had in the yard and the yard still was not in India. what do you think they thought about the covetous hair of the indio and coolie by the way. how much do you think they thought about the meanings of their wants until they became cannot haves and cannot have nots. what kind of brown touches burnt enough to make black. who among them was forced to remember their power and act?[2]

blood chorus

only water. not bread. only salt. not soap. only waiting. not want. only breathing. not hope. only offer. not gift. only levee. not lift. only hours. not shift. only air.[1]

we are light filtered lovingly, meaning we are dark. we are energy that sparks. we are heat that deepens pace. we are interior and face. we are back from outer space. we are evidence we are trace. we are gifted we are grace. we are growing out of place. we are waiting after waste. we are stardust after taste. we are eloquent in haste. we say it excessively. we. sculpted by destiny. we. wind call. the breath in me. we. here now so. let it be.[2]

us? we let the whales name us. deep with their moaning. we put our ears underwater and knew. we let the whales name us with their heat, their light, their bones around us. the smell of them, our need, our names were true.

us? it was the turtles named us. with the scraping of their walking, with our scraping out their insides. it was the turtles, not the eels, as they sunk and swam in water, as they danced like half-lit planets, as they lived inside the confines of their speed.

who? us? we lost our names in fires and when the boat crashed and the crop broke. we lost our names in stages of pronounce. we found new names in scripture and in force and in convenience. they taste like sand and silt inside our mouths.

me? i let them call me what they wanted to call me. what they saw. i let them say what first they felt to say. i didn't need a name, not last or first as far as i saw it. they said what they said. i let it stay.

you? we made your name from fragments. from memories and accidents. we made your name from longing and from lust. we made it up from TV shows, mythology and impulse. you keep it. you make it what you want.[3]

jobless? obviously there is work to be done. so it's not that.

jah bless? we don't know about that directly. but sure.

diablesse. now that we can talk about.

there are women among us. among you. who know more about their power than can be tolerated. so they do not aim for toleration. they go straight for love. the vein in the throat. they hug up close on those who fear them so no one can get a clear shot. no man can know for sure is it she or himself that smells like flowers in the middle of the night. we would call them workers because they do almost everything. we would call them gods because they do not ever die.[4]

sometimes we see it on the palms of our hands and it is there or it is not. or it is the routine redness of our hands pounding on stone to make it food, pounding on days to make them clean enough, clapping as if to wake the dead. it reddens us there. sometimes it is there. sometimes it is the blood of breaking through, the blood of someone else's birth, the blood of our own loss that lingers. our hands are washed in menstrual blood. they are not clean. they are complicit. involved in every birth and death. red is red ain't. red shadow red taint. red. blood red. the color of breath.[5]

we make flowers out of our own blood. we can put them in water.
we can put them in dirt. we can keep them and grow something else.
flower you.

we make love out of our own pain. the pain that comes. again. again.
we made you from our regular pain. our red and fleeting joy.

we grow blood out of our low accessible hearts. our stretched legs.
our belly parts. we take love from the part of the brain that don't
breathe.

we paint the world with the blood we keep. or leave.[6]

when we had bodies we were like trees. or was it coral? marked through time by layers under the skin. how many times we had been here. who we were looking for. what we came to do. what we came to undo. you could see it all. frequencies. allergies. who we used to know. what we wanted to forget. whether this time it would be hard or easy. what to say to put us on pause. what to say to move us to action. what you would say that would make us remember all the times we had been here and how it hurt. what you could say that would make us remember why we came back in the first place, and the second place, and the third place.

and this time.[7]

this is not the way it was supposed to be. all of us afraid to love you. you afraid to listen. this is not what you call free. it is forced on every side. we hide from it even in our laughter. this is not who you were gonna be. harried and afraid of ever after. we didn't want to have to project our dreams forward like this. we wanted to be happy right then. our own wildest dreams. right away. not waiting for death and vindication. you have to be a poet because of all that didn't happen. but if we'd had our way. really had our day. who knows what you'd be doing now.[8]

do you think we asked ourselves what was the meaning of our existence? what was our sound among the stars? what should we have done or not done by thirty-five? who could feel our impact on Mars? we didn't. we knew though that we should exist. and we kept each other alive like we had been here before. and we moved by the speed of light. meaning, often by the time anyone noticed us we were gone.[9]

at some point we all had to learn how to see the invisible. the unborn, the unremembered, the discounted, ourselves. we would have had to add the spirit to the air if it wasn't already thick with it. for us it was a matter of what you call love. thick relation. what you call ritual. repetitive action. we fed the gods that were ourselves by feeding each other. we made the sounds that were our angels by singing aloud. we proved the lie that lay in wait through touch in secret and in public. we made meaning out of the mess by what we did. and what we continued to do. once is a moment. twice is time travel. there are very few things that you are doing for the first time.[10]

some of us did what we had to do with shells and blood. and the moon was always there watching. the moon beyond the whiteness they imagined. the moon was with us always in her pull.

some of us did what we did not want to do with prayers and songs about imagined people when the real energy was all we needed. we opened ourselves to it anyway.

some of us sang below deck and the words we knew became less than words and more than sound and more air than air was under there.

some of us were silent about our power.

some of us taught it to our daughters in kitchens not our own.

some of us bought space for it with the fear and necessity of the birthing room.

some of us sent the unworthy to their tombs.

some of us were honored. some of us were feared.

some of us survived and some of us disappeared.

we are talking about what happened over the course of a thousand years.

in a certain way we are, each of us, still here.[11]

shop

first they had to acknowledge that they were not god. which was hard, because as far as they could see they had made everything and everyone. they had at least made anyone who had made anything. and for them in particular it was a felt contradiction. they should have inspired faith. they made the necessary unseen. they even made the invisible workers. they did the invisible work that kept those workers alive. they knew, but didn't say, that without them everything would fall apart. if only they could wish for it. if only they were not cursed with loving the deeply flawed world even as the praise for it was stolen off their shoulders in exchange for boulders added. even as the betrayals eroded their very bones and they stooped over. sometimes they watched apocalyptic movies and knew. if they were to let go, unknuckle this world, not one piece of human life could remain. and the power made them wise. it made them resourceful. it let them work miracles once in a while. but they still kept on making the world that would take everything from them. not only their labor but those they gave birth to. the world they made took the softness they nurtured and threw it against stone. and when their children were grown, the children blamed them personally. and what could they do, but sing about death and hope that their breath made it so, though their hands could not. what could they do but scream when another was shot, when the clothes that they bought burned in blood. what could they do but blame god for themselves and then repent and not forgive themselves and be spent and not live themselves and be rent and not with themselves and then get back to blaming themselves for not being god. what else?[1]

sometimes she listened, attracted by the sounds, the chants, especially the high-pitched parts. sometimes she made up rumors about them, just to think on them longer and see what anyone else knew. when she was a little girl she listened in the shop to what they said to each other in their own language. and understanding almost reached like high coconut in your own street. brown wisdom and pretty hair. she thought one day it would fall open at her feet and water the ground. but she never said anything about it. not even in her own thoughts. she just listened and looked and walked closer, in case.

under it all was what she knew. god should be a woman. all these worthless fool vicars. god should be a woman. then they'd see.[2]

great-great-grandmother durga or the better to slap you with

the sweat on her hands smoothes down her hair, which will become air and frizz again. she is sorting the have from the should be. separating the cans from the could be. this is her store. not in the sense of land. that's the bank and she has managed to contain the knowledge that she is behind on her payments to one bank employee with his own things to hide and think about. she has managed to contain the men who chase her behind with this counter. she has counted the cans and the staples and her hands. there are two of them. which makes it hard to smack away the waiting eyes of the lounging men and to smooth her flying-away hair again and to collect the money and protect her grandchild. she does it though. like the Indian gods of the shopkeeper from before. this is her store. not in the sense of keeping but of keeping away. she reserves the right to refuse anyone. and she does it, with spat words about their dark skin, their dirty feet, their reputations in the street. she has a child in here. who will not go the way of the other. she will not go the way of the mother. her daughter. her water. stolen by dirt. stay away until you have shoes and a shirt and a reason. *oona buying something or not?*

she sweeps again. too hot. and the girlchild is at school. with the hair she braided with these same smoothing hands which are not gentle. it takes sandpaper to smooth wood. it takes a rough hand to raise a child good. at least here it does. and she knows once in a while the people in the neighborhood steal. and that one drunk lingers near the door to sneak a feel, but what they will not take, is the grandchild she first furiously called a mistake. evidence of the theft of her daughter. and the original tainting of the water. the crime that got us here. and now that her daughter has disappeared, what now. but the sweat of her hands in her hair. the screaming at men that the girl in her care is not like them. with their dusty black need. the too quiet girlchild comes back and sits in the corner with her book. the men who were looking for work will soon come home to look for manhood again. there will never be a balance between what she sells and what's been took. she is not above sticking this broom in your face, she is not below chasing you out of this place. too hot. molten maybe. she is growing more hands.[3]

i am still screaming. i am not still. i am grieving. i am birthing. i

am not leaving. i am still here screaming. i am here pounding. i am
rage to break the rocks back open. rage the graves ungrounding. i
am sounding out the sounds that come after words and before them.
i am drowning in the dirt of what i've lost. i am tearing. i am claw-
ing, scratching, maiming. i am turning their skin into my own un-
taming. i am reaching for their generations. the mother within them
to unrape my life. i am breaking. i am smashing. i am purposefully
crashing glass against glass. spilling every form of spirit, breaking
loud so you can hear it. i am splintering the storeroom into flame. i
am your name. i am clearing with the washing wail of water. i am in
the river cleansing from the slaughter. i am blood on my own hands.
i am blood handed to daughters. i am sweat and every salt excretion,
river rock and mud creature. i am training i am teacher i am truth.
i am stomping, kicking, jumping, clapping. i am not surprised that
this still happens. i am here, arrange it. i am here reclaim it. i am here
with all your rage making the strange you need to change it.[4]

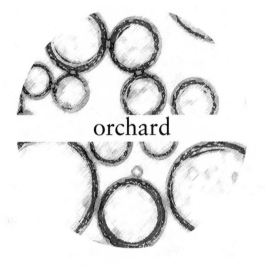

orchard

first they had to admit that they were not god. withstanding all the talk about the father. the monuments they wrote their names on stained with glass. their supposed rarity in the community. the stories they borrowed about self-making themselves. how necessary they seemed. while at the same time everything seemed to happen by magic (through the angel wives and secretaries they blessed with their light). first they had to really realize what money was not. after having money after having not had money for so long before that. they had to let go the lie that they had told themselves in such a disciplined and consistent way that it had actually led to having money. they had to learn that having money did not make them god and the gods they had worshiped for their money before them were also not god in the first place. they had to see for themselves what money could not do. and when they came back to what they had had before money and in some cases after, their bodies, when they came back to those backs that had been traded for money, as money, when they came back to back-breaking labor and being broke they had to also unlearn that their bodies made them god. regardless of the magical seed and what the women said to try to keep them. regardless of the sons and daughters everywhere. despite how they had endured what should have not been possible to endure. despite how they had made what should have been impossible to make. despite how their hands really felt like someone had nailed them, had nailed them to the crisis. they had to learn that the ongoing sacrifice of their bodies was not holy. it left a hole. like their fathers before them. and three days later it was work again and also for the whole three days between. the interval of three losing its magic, because whatever they did it didn't make them free. first they had to admit they were not god, how they had learned god. god how they had cursed god. god how they had shouted out in vain and no one came. god how they had welded metal into their own names and hit the ground with it. and it wasn't the ground that broke. it was their hearts. so they called out for their mothers. that was the start.[1]

who were you as a boy child among boy children and caring sisters who didn't care what you did but who would care for whomever you did it to. who were you as a boy child among other boy children and sisters and a mother who did everything, who was all day doing everything, washing everything, feeding everyone. did you ever see her eat. what about your father? did you ever see him feed her a treat. bring her a special orange maybe and peel it for her, offering her a section directly into her mouth as she kept washing or sorting or stirring. or was all that over by the time you would have noticed. who were you as a boy child among boy children and sisters and a mother and a father who did everything. who told you to follow only if you could keep up. who made you feel what? small or powerful? empty or entitled? did you want to be like him or did his burning hands make you crave another type of dirty work. what did he say to you that you remembered? or was it work over words between the two of you? who were you as a boy child among boy children following your father claiming shoes that you would not fit into though there were no other shoes. who were you as a boy child among boy children and sisters and a mother and a father who died and left after you already left. who were you as a boy child among boy children and parents and sisters who had already left and children of your own and a wife who went dancing who ultimately didn't need you and even cars and trucks that wouldn't stay the same after a while. who were you as a boy child among boy children calling themselves men. all of you at the Jamaican clubs and churches in Hartford, Connecticut, calling yourselves men among men in the men's choir, in the cold place where everyone you knew and everything you ate and everywhere you went was still West Indian. who were you as a boy child among boy children calling themselves men except when you would laugh and call each other home, crying out, "boy!!!"[2]

it is only right that you should listen for a minute. for a proverb or something. for me to talk so fast you can barely hear it, like if i was painting while running away. like if i myself didn't trust my impact. maybe i didn't. maybe i didn't see how me being me in particular would impact anyone in my life. maybe i didn't think that me being me in particular was enough. or was good at all. or maybe i thought if i was just generic, you know, light-skinned Jamaican man writ large, the category would share the weight of my behavior and the good and necessary would still get through. i didn't think i could know you, didn't really think you could know me. and now what do you have to use?

what you know about me most is what i watched on TV. or what it was like to watch TV beside me. and maybe i wanted you to see that the people on Court TV and *Judge Judy* and *Judge Hatchett* and all the other judge shows were worse than me. more worthy of judgment and so careless for people's lives. or maybe i was waiting to see how you would find compassion for them. find compassion for me, careless as i have been. powerless as i feel to fix it. what can i say now that i'm not in this cage called light-skinned Jamaican man of privilege and paranoia. what i can say now is call in the judge. bring me to judgment now. because i knew it would never be a bearded god i'd face. it would be the women i left behind.

call me to court. call me to count all the things i let happen and didn't do, all the things i did because we do them, all the questions i didn't ask. all the collateral damage from my lack of specificity, from my floating downstream, from my neutrality in the face of what destroys us. make a mahogany gavel and find some surface. slam it down.

or i will just be here. waiting for the sound of your footsteps, your robe. waiting for the theme music and the uniformed bailiff. waiting for my turn. waiting on you. waiting to rise.[3]

like you i woke up in the dark. but i was reaching for animals, trying to beat the heat. like you sunrise usually found me in the middle of doing something. i didn't call it prayer, but i did believe that if i did it every day we would exist. i would exist. the you i couldn't imagine would have a chance. you don't know about my mother. my father. my grandfather. people who would have thought my never-frostbitten ears a dream. people who wouldn't have known that stolen land could be so, loving. everything we had out there, we had to keep it alive. including each other. in the dark sometimes i was midwife. milkmaid. machine. somewhere in there a man. brown is relative. you are more brown than i was after all the sun of the equator. after all the son of some black woman as loving as land. and i believed in trees and watched their skin, inheritor of so much space that you have never been to, have you. oh but i met you once. brown like a baby next to me. i was brown like an old man then. in the middle of the day. and the skin of the orange tree was important. there is something i would teach you about it. if we both had been in any condition to take a walk or listen, i would have put your hand to the trunk of the tree. there is something for you to know there. i could have been the one to tell you.

but instead i gave your grandmother sweet oranges, so she could feel special under the bored light of my son. and i hear she planted her own orange tree and passed it on to you. not the tree itself or the land it was on, but the sweet that comes from brown. you greet me still, greedy for stillness, early in the morning.[4]

you can see why they would believe in faeries in all that green. the sloping hills, even the mountains round like they had been there for-ever. where even the dead were walking distance from home. even if they had walked a very great distance to die. and they made their words round too. brewed drink too strong and then prided them-selves on being strong enough to drink far too much of it. and they drank until they could see them, the faerie folk, see themselves in all their fairness or ruddy and cold. but after all it was an island too with its own volcanoes to remember. when i dream sometimes i don't know which island, until i wake up in all this heat.[5]

it is not about what i wanted. i didn't give myself space to want. i didn't want myself space to give. well actually. i wasn't given the type of space that you would want to give to someone else. but sometimes. when i was standing in the kitchen listening to them eat and wondering if anyone would come by hungry that i could feed. sometimes. when i was stretching the clothes out onto the bushes to dry in the sun. sometimes. when i was noticing the gap between what a daughter or granddaughter or niece knew and what she needed to know. sometimes. when i was chasing them out of my kitchen. sometimes. in the garden wondering about which seeds would grow and which would rest. sometimes. when despite my practiced efficiency, my systems for perfection, my full as possible attention, something still spilled in my house. sometimes i did imagine, just for a moment in between washing. just for a moment snapping the peas. just for a moment washing the dirt a third time out of the cuffs of my husband's sleeves. i did imagine space. what it would be like for one of you, not me, of course not me, to have space enough to not think about what fire, what boil, what next sweet piece of toil did you belong to. and if it wasn't something i could teach by example to your mother's cousin Joy. and it if wasn't something i could temper in your grandmother Joyce. and if it wasn't the same as reusing enough cloth to save enough store money to send my girls away to nursing school in foreign. then maybe i could cook it up and feed it through. but all the peas i planted and fed would be peas again too never mind flowers. and i didn't have so much as an hour to remember it. though i did earn sleep. sometimes briefly i would dream. and it seemed strange. a person like you. with time. and empty hands. so full of all the possible things to care about in the excess of my most sparing specific days. i mean whales? it's me still sometimes in awe of the dishwasher, telling you not to wait, and to stack everything now. and pick that saucer up on your way. and cook everything in that beautiful refrigerator. and don't let the oranges just sit there. don't you know what it actually takes to make something grow. it takes every attention. but then you don't. and really i don't want you to. i stand here and watch the strange things that you do while i wash and then wring out the clouds. in my way i am proud. and i send you a push just to save you some time. just to see what you'll do.[6]

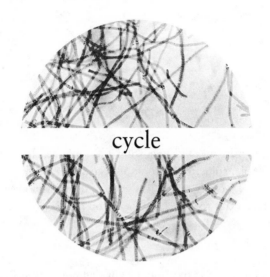

cycle

what the star said to the earth:

sometimes i wish i was like you. solid and findable. thick and round. cool and stable. sometimes i look at you when you don't think i'm looking at you. you are there in the dark of me and i see mysteries that make me want to sing. but would you hear?

what the earth said to the star:

sometimes i wish i was like you. bright and hot. fast as light and always lit. seen even after you are gone. i wish that people wished on me like how they wish on you. make you into prophecy. claim you as their origin when i am still right here. sometimes i listen to you when you think i am not listening to you and i don't know how to feel about your song. so i tilt. so i keep spinning. so i stay around.[1]

it turns. that's what we know. and supposedly it is too slow for any-one to feel it. that's an underestimation, made by men who ignore the impact of cycles on their own dull dizzying days. work around work around work around. if only the ground was something to hold on to. i would hold your heartbeat in my head. if only this constant dragging didn't mean that we all would end up dead.[2]

southern fruit of high planted stalk. of wind-carried seed of unan-
swered need. brazen root of unhurried trees of foundations found
and broke through. bright leaves of won't you, split crook of don't
you, raised welt of shown true the black. your back.

you're back. the black true shone. of welt raise you. don't. of crook
split. you. want of leaves bright. through broke and found founda-
tions. of trees unhurried. of root brazen. need unanswered. of seed
carried. wind of stalk planted. high of fruit. southern.[3]

saving the planet

mostly water. you. the planet. mostly dark. the matter and energy. only understood through its impact. and its persistent incomprehensibility to those afraid to understand. the things they will do to water. do with water. for money. the things you do with water. the gallons you flush everyday. mellow yellow notwithstanding.

not with standing rock.

remember. water is like other forms of energy. it transforms. it does not disappear. and once the water from the fire hoses took the bark off the trees and the skin off the brave brown people. once they watched it on TV, the water splashing off the Sunday-dressed children. their sweat, their showers, their tears, their spit, their wet beds in the morning were charged. we are charged. any of us who sweat, who shower, who drink water. all of us are charged.

remember. you come from a people who not so long ago didn't use water that way, that gave back to this land that sweats god's tears of joy.

now? none of us are clean.[1]

honey. follow the honey. that means your own sticky fingers to the jar. edges uncontainable, crystal into glass grooves. rivers of excess to the counter. glue of sweet knotting up the cloth. and of course the divine dissolution in your dark leaves of tea. the destiny of your throat. the heat holding medicine, clearing you for song. even if it's the song of sitting here typing all day long. follow the honey.

what happens when you drop a glass jar on a brick floor and the sharp is slow the coming apart reluctant like your heart. brave sharp and shattered pieces held together only by the holding pattern of gold. the thick sweat of whole communities of bees. the crystalline structure remembered. what is happening in your shaking hands when you drop it like that. your glass heart holding years of work. droppéd now onto this brick floor of day.

what happens when you explode a plastic squeeze container in your luggage. compartmentalized only by unhelpful netting and holy grocery bags. and everything you wore or wanted to wear is stuck, is claimed is uncleaned unwipeable not even with your mouth. and you imagine. if you could put on all your sweet and hardening clothes at the same time. and immerse yourself like tea into a cup big enough to hold you, hot enough to melt you back to use. you could be you again. first-degree burnt brown and reddening skin notwithstanding. you could be who you really are. a bag of leaves vulnerable in mesh. a stapled pouch of leaving. ouch. the wonder being how none of the broken pieces are small enough to fit through the tiny holes in you.

your pores so much smaller than they feel. and how the dark bleeds out and fills the water. and how you press yourself to porcelain hoping nothing will be left of flavor. hoping everything to be learned has finally come out. but that's not what it's about and the press is never total.

what happens when you pilfer packets to sneak onto the plane. you keep them in all the pockets of your computer bag. you quite recklessly stash them and forget them. because you hate that feeling of rejection when a place has hot water but no honey. lemon but no sweet. imagine. and so you stash it. such a volatile substance that it's rumored to kill babies. such a staining africanizable substance that it is only allowed aboard planes in tiny quantities. a stolen substance from the geometric homes of drones designed to stab you. what a strange idea of safety you have sutured in this mess. you put it in all your pockets because honey,

you might need it in this bitter world yet.[2]

get into a circle so you can see each other. see the part of yourself that you want to avoid. you have to see it. feel it in the radius of your heart so we can grow. no one deserves to live in a broken world without a circle, sutured together by denials. what do you think about that. a world without its circles remade every day by breaking, taking and looking away. a world so fearfully made we cannot look in each other's eyes. a world so carelessly held that we shape lies and reshape them in the repetition of our minds. and cannot sleep. can fall and not catch each other. so when they say the argument is circular? they don't know circle like we know circle. they don't know circle at all. they should keep her name out they mouth truth be told.[3]

she asked them to move their hands. move their hands like they were making detail out of air. move their hands like they were moving their own spirits through the eye of a needle. and everyone else's eyes, rich with intention. she asked them to hold on to things invisible. so small as to seem impossible. she asked them to grow those things. link them to each other. recognize that they were powerful because of their pattern. their relation. their elation on discovering they were everywhere. she asked them to work with their breathing thick like strands of hair. to braid their breathing across bodies into care. she asked if they would listen. not only with their minds, their allied open hearts. but also would they listen with their hands.[4]

we told you. a circle. preferably blessed by a grove of trees. ideally next to a major body of water. so the ground, while temporary, knows roots. so the water, though always moving, has depth for what we doing. if you have hands, find a way to hold hands. if you have eyes, use them to look at each other with love. as close to the beginning as possible, bring your folks, that would be us, the beyond bodied. as if we have nothing to do but work for you. really we are nothing but the work you still have yet to do. don't forget that.

if you want, strategically time yourselves to meet the sun or the moon or smaller lights like candles or the smiles of children. or do it at a time when people are remembering love. or do it at a time when people have done this before. or do it in a place where enough people have cried that you feel it, a major body of water in the air. or in a place where people have been brave and burned with their belief in change. or in a stolen place among the many stolen places that will not keep. or just a place comfortable enough that there will be old people and children. remember food or the promise of food. or no one will come. not even us.

a circle. you can choose a number like nine or twenty-one or seven, but accept the number that arrive. it will be good in some cases to have people you have known a while. in some cases to have people you don't know at all. and sometimes it will just be you, the you you becoming, the you you been, the you you lust for, the you you blaming, the you you need, the you you have, the you you haven't thanked yet and the you before and after that (meaning us). however the gathering, we'll be there.

it's enough.[5]

we let you think you choose. you choose like wind chooses. like water chooses. like heat chooses to move. its path intersecting with everything. its hands touching trees or sand. we let you think you move. you move as much as land. meaning only by an inner heat older than you by centuries. you can think you choose. but we would say you notice. or you don't.[6]

staying

when wind and water love you, you can do anything. you can let yourself be buried. you can fly. when wind and water rush to meet you anywhere you go, you can go anywhere. or you can stay. when wind and water clamor for your face with rushing secrets, you can forget or remember or know. when wind and water teach you, touch you, crash into your skin, you are preserved. or you can grow. if wind and water love you like you say they really love you, you don't need a life jacket or wings. if wind and water taught you what you think they really taught you, you can let go of your places and your things. if wind and water got you, that means wind and water got you; there is no little bit about their lashing love. if wind and water want you, you are here for wind and water. it don't matter if you ever call it love.[1]

when you faint, go back to that circle of people. that circle of people, you know who they are. you might not know their names, you can trust all their faces, they will take you to places that have what you need. if you fail, channel back to that circle of people, that circle of people who share all you do. those spirits dressed up in the glow of your victory, the light of your longing they will be there still. when you want, go home to that circle of people. that circle of people laying hands and saying prayers. anytime recognize it, that circle of people. they are always there. you are theirs.[2]

add it up. years of sand and salt. that way you have of breathing the calmest parts of the ocean. poems, half-memorized and forgiven. belief that you can float. enough peace to actually float, at least a few minutes at a time. a place to go and eat and cry when you have lost too much weight to stay lost. the possibility of a personal writing retreat. the possibility of a group writing retreat. a place to come be with the moon. the subtle rewriting of spirit prompted by the month-long sound of the ocean. the mothering it invites with gratitude. the lagoon dreams. the names in Hutson's book. the beautiful painting of the woman giving birth to the world. the necklace that opened your voice beyond lifetimes. that way of wearing exactly what you want to wear. an intimate knowledge of impermanence. humility. lack of entitlement. as every day the ocean takes the land away. as other things you thought you could stand on erode. an instinct for ceremony any time any place. the poetry trained readiness for miracles on a day. the space to love yourself. the time to come ask questions. the patience to sit with old people, to hear the same stories and find something new. the ear to listen past shouting. the lung control to shout when you need to. the words. the rapport with birds. the oneness with whales. the recognition of sails as nothing without breath. the bridge across death. the geography of clouds. eye contact with horizon. the site-specific ability to turn off your phone. the illusion of security. the illusion of home for what it offered. the thousands of footsteps proffered. your signature in sand. we give what we give in form. and its form is not land.[3]

burn the trash, the dry discarded piles will teach you again how black is air. how black is water. black as the plastic foot-tub mosquito hub. pour it out. how black is land? black enough that it can be bought and sold. black enough that it can understand. how black is the storm that comes from West Africa every year at carnival time. how black are the hands that clear the brush and rebuild the broken buildings again. how black is the sand of the volcanic neighbor the coral undercarriage the remnant tar. how black is the airborne salt that leathers your skin, corrodes your car. how black are the days you spend sweet-talking spenders and bending your forehead to ground. how black are the ways you wind up here. how black the staying sound.[4]

you were trying to go back to a place before knowledge. you keep try-
ing to go back there as you sit and breathe and chant. and best case,
all you know is that you know. on a good day all you know is you
are known. on a Sunday you might feel known and held and know
that. but underneath that. keeping you up. keeping you waking up
and meeting us here. keeping you scrawling and calling our names
is another knowing. how can you know that you are unknowable?
how can you know that you cannot know that which knows you
best. how can you best note the knowing that won't happen here.
nope. how can you know the unknowing that is ultimately the test.
see. you don't see. that's what's black about it.[5]

put it in the food. the tears. and save on salt. put it in the plants. the
screams. and repay breath. put it under your nails. the filth. and help
the clothes. put it in the work. she learned. to outrun death.

put it in the sky. the sweat. and become clouds. put it in the sand. the
edge and cut him there. put it in the trees. the sin. and invite wind.
put it in the wind. and learn. to live again.

put it in their mouths. the prayers. and save them still. put it in their
hands. the love. and let them build. put it in their eyes. the truth. and
let them cry. put it in their hearts. your heaven. and do not die.[6]

letting go

there is no reason to believe you would be supernaturally strong. except you survived. and told the tale. except you expected to survive. and didn't listen for what they couldn't say. well, that's one version of superpowers right? like on TV where the extraplanetary leaches into your skin. where your extreme usefulness to the populace robs you only one thing. your ability to breathe. only one thing. everyone you love. only one thing. your right to say who you are in the middle of the day. only one thing. the luxury not to wear the costume.

stop. there is every reason to stop thinking. there is every reason to stop thinking you are god. there is every reason to stop thinking. you are god. stop. thinking. you are here. stop thinking. you are god. you are god because you are still here. there is nothing here that is not still god. stop. there is nothing. supernatural. about. that.[1]

what if you were reborn with nothing to prove. you didn't need any-
thing named after you or anyone to notice. what if you were reborn
with nothing to give and you gave it happily and didn't seek more.
what if you were born living just the one life, with no pressure to
erase or uplift those that came before you. what if you were born
just to dance and sing and cry with the ones who adored you and the
ones who deplored you. what if you were born with keys and found
nothing was locked and your spirit wasn't shocked by open doors.
what if you were born with absolutely nothing to prove. nothing to
reach for or to store. what if you were born with nothing, less than
nothing. meaning, more.[2]

there is no rejection. there is calling. may you always be available to your purpose.

there is no proof. there is presence. may you always be all of where you are.

there is no problem. there is practice. practice letting go.[3]

what if you stopped thinking you were blood, and let yourself be water. what if you stopped thinking you were water and let yourself be air. what if you stopped thinking you were air and let yourself be dirt. what if you stopped thinking you were safe and left it there.

what if
what if you did
stop thinking
what if
what if you
let yourself be
what if
you were
blood, water, breath, and leaving
what if
you were
free[4]

you could read about it. all of it. read yourself to sleep. you could dream about it, metaphorically and keep about a tenth of what you see. you could look for us literally in the shapes of the clouds or the sounds of the sea. you could sweat us home, you could dance us up. but have you tried this? stop. just be.[5]

when you carry it. it pushes on your shoulders. it pulls your muscles down. it slowly teases them apart from tendon. you tend towards the spineless when you carry all that wrong.

when you carry it. it takes up your hands with invisible shaking. it is taking away their openness to something else.

when you hold it. it gets bolder atop you, it learns how most easily to stop you from the you of your momentum. it strains you at the septum and you push against your own teeth as if you don't need them.

when you let them. fear makes burrows in your spirit. shortcuts so you hear it louder than your purpose now.

when you cow. when you walk between the bars to the destiny of craws and grind and crushing. when you ignore the screams and silence at the end of all the pushing. when you bow to that which don't deserve the blush the gushing. when you pray to idle plods about the burden. you keep on hurting. you and everyone you shove.

and when you love. you let it go. you put it down. you show your shoulders what to do with sky. and love is how. and love is when. and love is why.[6]

acknowledgments

Love is why. (The rule is love.) I acknowledge all my relations. I acknowledge all. My relations. Thank the air and the earth and the heat and the water for converging in me. Thank all the directions for meeting me everywhere. Thank my grandfather Jeremiah Gumbs for remembering poems. Thank my grandmother Lydia Gumbs for practicing community as design and listening to dolphins. Thank my great-grandmother Augusta Carty for living a black and blackening love. Thank my great-grandfather Paul McKenzie for growing oranges. Thank my great-grandmother Sarah McKenzie for growing community and family. Thank my grandmother Joyce McKenzie for nurturing love. Thank my great-great-great-grandmother Georgianna for offering embrace. Thank my great-great-grandmother Rebecca for protecting women and girls from sexual violence. Thank my great-grandmother Eugenia for going where she needed to go. Thank my great-grandfather Aubrey Jones for recognition. Thank my grandfather Joseph McKenzie for his proverbs.

Thank my cousin Hutson for writing down the history. Thank my Aunt Una Gumbs for remembering the lineage. Thank my Uncle Alan Gumbs and Aunt Lisa Gumbs for holding space for memory and miracles. Thank my Uncle Duane and Aunt Carol for feeding and caring for generations. Thank my Uncle Keith for loving the people. Thank my Aunt Isabel for her faith. Thank my cousin Kyle McKenzie for insisting on experience. Thank my cousin Sean McKenzie for telling the truth even if it's a whisper. Thank my Uncle Fred for mystery and a chemistry set. Thank my mother in love Anne Wallace for revolutionary mothering and grandmothering. Thank my father in love Waylon Wallace for genealogy and genius. Thank my sister in love Erica Wallace for remembering healing power. Thank my sister in love Laura Wallace for continuing to write. Thank my nephew Elijah Michael for an open heart. Thank my niece Taylor Michael for good questions. Thank my nephew Lazarus Michael for vulnerability and freedom. Thank my nephew Jayden Wallace for attentive love. Thank my nephew Jorden Wallace for honest storytelling. Thank my nephew Jaleel Wallace for old soul reminders. Thank my sister Kyla Day-Fletcher for the shared journey. Thank my brother in love Nic Fletcher for sharing generations. Thank my nephew Logan Day-Fletcher for being best friends with everyone at once. Thank my nephew Lucas Day-Fletcher for just being here. Thank my cousin Justin Gumbs for helping me learn compassion. Thank little Jeremiah for rebirth. Thank my cousin Victoria Ruan for keeping a song alive inside. Thank my cousin in love Davan Ruan for retaining and sharing the superpowers. Thank my baby cousin Dorian for showing up just in time. Thank my cousin Branden Gumbs for being an artist. Thank my brother Jared Gumbs for reflection. Thank my brother Seneca Morin for my dreams. Thank my sister Ariana Good for the next generation. Thank my brother in love Andrew Good for loving whales. Thank my niece McKenzie Marie Good for re-introducing me to my inner child. Thank my niece Penelope McClive Good for teaching me a new language.

Thank my father, Clyde Gumbs, for my belief that everything can change. Thank my mother, Pauline McKenzie, for my loved and loving life.

Thank my ancestors named. Thank my ancestors unnamable.

Thank my mentormother Cheryll Greene for the eyes of an editor and the soul of a sister. Thank my mentorauntie Cynthia Brown for never leaving anyone behind. Thank my namesake Alexis De Veaux for making the name a prayer and a practice. Thank my cherished Sokari Ekine for making breathing and spirit portable. Thank you queen fairy emeritus Courtney Reid-Eaton for modeling magic. Thank you Omi Osun for the power of the present moment. Thank you Sharon Bridgforth for doing your love work and for every invitation. Thank you M. Jacqui Alexander for infinite modalities of listening. Thank you Soul Brother Eric Pritchard for love without limit.

Thank you sister-comrade Aishah Simmons for breaking silences. Thank you M. NourbeSe Philip for transforming the way I look and live through language. Thank you exemplary "somebody" Jeannette Bronson for your devotion. Thank you sister Ebony Noelle Golden for early advice on this series and for its future as durational performances. Thank you sister Yashna Maya Padamsee for teaching me to breathe. Thank you sister Leah Lakshmi Piepzna-Samarsinha for keeping me honest. Thank you sister Adrienne Maree Brown for living your truth and bringing me with you. Thank you sister Walidah Imarisha for being the baddest good sista a sista can have. Thank you sister Kara Urqhart Green for love and laughter. Thank you sister Janelle Edwards Steward for love and faith. Thank you sister Savannah Shange for the all ages of revolution. Thank you beacon Toshi Reagon for sower and harvest. Thank you brotherunclereverend Marvin K. White for your love and the sacred word. Thank you Baba Chuck Davis for making Durham a portal for dance that could heal me. Thank you Mama Nayo Watkins for building a community that could perform memory and possibility at the same time.

Thank you to Shinnecock elders Quita Sullivan, Lance Gumbs, and Denise Silva Dennis for helping me listen.

Gratitude to my intellectual family of origin and growth for nurturing my interest and my excess and my soul. There are too many people to name, but thank you especially to my high school teachers Donna Ellwood and Catherine Tipton and everyone at Paideia. Thank you to Monica Miller, Farah Jasmine Griffin, Mignon Moore, Sharon Harris, Vivian Taylor, Rosalind Rosenberg, Thaddeaus Russell, and Jennie Kassanoff at Barnard College and Columbia University. Thank you Marcellous Blount. You live forever. Thank you Maurice Wallace, Wahneema Lubiano, Karla Holloway, Fred Moten, Michelene Crichlow, Mark Anthony Neal, Ian Baucom, Tina Campt, Sharon Holland, Deborah Thomas, John Thomas, and Priscilla Wald for your time at Duke University and for deciding to support my strangest propositions. Thank you for creating precedents and not precincts.

I am grateful for the scholars and activists who supported me beyond institutional affiliation. Thank you for your generosity, Hortense Spillers, Ruth Nicole Brown, Saidiya Hartman, Tavia Nyong'o, Michelle Wright, Layli Phillips Marpayan, Beverly Guy-Sheftall, Akasha Hull, Barbara Smith, Demita Frazier, Margo Okazawa-Rey, Barbara Ransby, Ruthie Gilmore, and Mendi + Keith Obadike. I acknowledge with gratitude and love the community of scholars who made my immersion in the work of Sylvia Wynter and Caribbean studies possible. Thank you first of all to Brent Edwards for telling me about Sylvia Wynter and then mailing the essay "Ethno or Socio Poetics" to my house. Thank you Katherine McKittrick for *Demonic Grounds* which I bought in the Toronto Women's Bookstore and which provided me with my first comprehensive bibliography of Wynter, and for your loving and tireless dedication and loyalty to Wynter's work. Thank you Deb Thomas, Tina Campt, and the committee of those multiple Diasporic Hegemonies conferences for introducing me to M. Jacqui Alexander, Alyssa Trotz, Reinaldo Walcott, and Andrea Smith without whom this work would be unimaginable. Thank you Anthony Bogues for organizing a symposium and celebration of Wynter at the University of the West Indies at Mona. Thank you Carole Boyce Davies and everyone on the committee of the Association of Caribbean Writers and Scholars for featuring Sylvia Wynter as a major speaker at the conference in Miami. Thank you Nick Mitchell for sharing everything you have shared and for supporting Wynter's continued work. Thank you David Stein for offering to bring me to meet Wynter in California even though I couldn't do it. Thank you Hyacinth Simpson, Ivy Wilson, Donette Francis, and Christian Campbell for encouraging my earliest writing about the Caribbean/as a Caribbean scholar. Thank you Annie Paul for generously guiding my first scholarly visit to Jamaica. Thank you Ronald Cummings for telling me who Dionne Brand is and for being a brother in this work forever. Thank you Omise'eke Tinsley for bringing the sweetness, fierceness, and clarity of water to us all. Thank you cousin Matt Richardson for teaching me that we can transform our Lesser Antilles narratives and family lines. Thank you Angelique Nixon for your dedication to our queer Caribbean contribution and the legacy of the Lorde. Thank you Rosamond King for exemplifying intergenerational accountability and brave critical poetics. Thank you Erna Brodber for welcoming me immediately. Thank you Merle Hodge for remembering me unapologetically. Thank you Velma Pollard for ferocious reclamation. Thank you Dionne Brand for making it impossible for me to not write about the Caribbean and diaspora. Thank you Audre Lorde for making it possible for me to write about anything. Thank you Gloria Joseph for helping to bring me home to Audre and myself. Thank each of you for helping me find my way back.

I am grateful for my first feminist literary community, Charis Books/Charis Circle, in Atlanta, Georgia. Thank you for creating a space of attention and love for us, Linda Bryant. Thank you Errol Raymond Anderson and Beatrice Sullivan for traveling with me forever in the light of what our words make possible.

I am grateful for my spiritual teachers and spiritual community who have deepened my ancestral listening and activated my oracle consciousness. Thank you Ifalade Tashia Asanti, Ifasade Oyade (Queen Hollins), Osunnike Ankh, Koleoso Karade, and all the beloved practitioners in Ile Ori Ogbe Egun and the Institute of Whole Life Healing (Many Paths One Truth).

I am grateful to my Brilliance Remastered family who support my life as an independent scholar and make it possible. Thank you for thinking with me the whole time I was writing and editing this. Special love to those who co-created ceremony with me during this period's Brilliance Remastered Intensives. Our ancestors are gathered. Our spirits are kindred. Love to Mel Monoceros, Jessica Marie Johnson, Tina Zafreen, Natalie Clark, Laura Sullivan, Bianca Laureano, Iyatunde Folayan, Rockie Gilford Stepter, Nicole Wilson, Nzingha Tyehemba, Mankwe Ndosi, Tamiko Beyer, Daphne Jayapal, Patricia Torres, Lydia Kelow-Bennett, Matice Moore, Naima Lowe, Auset O'Neal, Stephanie Latty, Lorraine Warren, Marie Varghese, D Smith, Jamilah Bradshaw, Agatha Roa, Grace Nichols, Alexis Flanagan, Ayana Omilade Flewellen, and Tala Khanmalek. You are answered prayers.

I am grateful for my community of Women of Color Media Makers who taught me how to be a community-accountable scholar in a digital world. Thank you for bringing us together, Nadia Abou-Karr. Thank you for loving me, Sydette Harry, Susana Adame, Meagan "La Mala" Ortiz, Lisa Factora-Borchers, Stacey Milbern, Adela Nieves, Noemi Martinez, Fabiola Sandoval, Elena Rose, and Rosa Cabrera. May we continue to seize the world around us with our freedom.

I am grateful to my Durham community for supporting me while I was writing this: Aleese Moore-Obih, Faith Holseart, Beth Bruch, Maya Freelon, Zaina Alsous, Destiny Hemphill, Michelle Lanier, Eden Segbefia, Lana Garland, Manju Rajendran Mariel Eaves, Tema Okun, and Lynne Walters. I am grateful to our Earthseed Family, Cristina River Chapman, Zulayka Santiago, Kifu Faruq, Courtney Woods, Santos Flores, Tahz Rufus Walker, Justin Robinson, Corre Robinson, and the babies! I am grateful to SpiritHouse and Warrior Healer Fam, especially Ade Toyesi Nia Wilson, Solanke Omimuyegun Racheal Derello, Afiya Carter, Osunfunke Omisade Burney-Scott, Kriti Sharma, Mya Hunter, Tia Hall, Matthias Pressley, Michelle Gonzales-Green, Hadassah Jones, Naeemah Kelly, Assata Goff, Sekou Goff, Heather Lee, Paul (Yusef) Newman, Adele Rose Luebke, Taj Scott, and everyone in the SpiritHouse and Warrior Healer families. Eternal love to our young brilliant ancestors Umar Muhammed and Brian Wiley and their families.

I am grateful to my Carriacou Sisters who attended and organized the Spiral Lab "Take My Jewel for Light Retreat." Thank you Karma Mayet Johnson and Shelley Nicole for listening to spirit and creating the space. Thank you Donna Hope, Katherine Johnson, Cousin Cindy McKenzie, Jani White, Denise Mervis, Tammy Brown, and Paulette Jones.

I am grateful to my Twin Cities community for supporting me while I finalized this manuscript. Thank you especially to Zenzele Isoke for inviting me to hold the visiting 2017–19 Winton Chair at University of Minnesota and for offering sistering and literal warmth. Thank you to Naimah Petigny for priceless research assistance and grounded sistering during this time. Much love to Mankwe Ndosi, Erin Sharkey, Signe Harriday, Junauda Petrus, Zoe Hollomon, ShaVunda Brown, Ego Ahaiwe, Ngowo Nasah, Frida Martin, Ananya Chatterjea, Alessandra Williams, Katie Robinson, Adrienne Doyle, Sally Nixon, Dana Suttles, Shannon Gibney, Danielle Mkali, Beverly Cottman, Cherisse Turner, Paige Reynolds, Kiara Jackson, Shannon Miller, Nasreen Mohamed, and Joi D. Lewis. Thank you to the cast of Sharon Bridgforth's *Dat Black Mermaid Man Lady*, Pavielle French, Florinda Bryant, Aimee Bryant, and Kenyai O'Neal for teaching me to read a different way. Thank you to Marcus Young, Mire Regulus, and the Don't You Feel It Too Cohort!

Thank you to the team at Duke University Press, especially Ken Wissoker for your supportive listening and for believing in me beyond the work. Thank you everyone who has helped midwife this triptych, especially Olivia Polk, Nicole Campbell, Jade Brooks, Jessica Ryan, Heather Hensley, Chad Royal, Laura Sell, Michael McCullough, and Liz Smith. Thank you cousin Stephanie Gomez for your smile and for slanging the books! Thank you Nina Oteria Foster for your insightful questions about this manuscript. Thank you to the anonymous reviewers for advocating for me with love and specificity.

Parts of this work were published under different names with slight differences in *Ecotone*, *Indiana Review*, *Scalawag*, *Meridians*, and *Feminist Formations*. Gratitude to the editors at each of those journals.

I shared parts of this work at Stellar Masses, a project of Philadelphia Contemporary. Thank you dear sister Yolanda Wisher for creating a sacred space and for your curation as divination.

I shared parts of this work at Evergreen College as the 2017 Evans Chair. Thank you Naima Lowe for inviting me into your community and for your brave and loving stand for your students.

I am grateful to the divine Cauleen Smith for allowing her art to grace the cover of this book. I am grateful to my sister dreamer artist Soraya Jean-Louis McElroy for creating the portal cover of *M Archive*. I am grateful to the brilliant Kenyatta A. C. Hinkle for creating the haunting cover of *Spill*. I am grateful to my love Sangodare for periodic-table illustrations in *M Archive* that allowed people to become scientists in time to read this book and for your oceanic illustrations in this text.

To Sylvia Wynter—thank you for your bravery. Thank you for the size and sincerity of your vision. Thank you for every word.

And most of all (again) to my first and last reader, thank you Sangodare (aka JDub) for the unconditional love that makes me brave enough to write every day whether or not it will make sense to anyone ever.

notes

request

1   genre-specific mode of material provisioning, "Human Being as Noun?," 18.

commitment

1   the intervention as the manifesto of the ceremony found, "Human Being as Noun?," 7.

instructions

1   representation of origins, "Human Being as Noun?," 34.

opening

1   But who are "we"?, "Ethno or Socio Poetics," 80.
2   organizing system, "No Humans Involved," 53.
3   gender is not a noun, "Human Being as Noun?," 8 (citing Judith Butler).
4   third, the rise, "On How We Mistook the Map for the Territory," 4.
5   ethnically rechristened African-American Studies, "On How We Mistook the Map for the Territory," 5.
6   autopoetic or self-organizing living system, "No Humans Involved," 58.
7   must, "Rethinking 'Aesthetics,'" 271.

whale chorus

1 landed, "Ethno or Socio Poetics," 81.
2 ostensibly *indubitably* and *self-determined* nature of consciousness, "Human Being as Noun?," 16.
3 postmodern intra-western, "Human Being as Noun?," 5.
4 especially since we ourselves are of this type, "Human Being as Noun?," 1.
5 The Dream of Reason, citing David Pagels, in "No Humans Involved," 68.

remembering

1 abstraction, "Ethno or Socio Poetics," 86.
2 differently motivating the respective categories, "No Humans Involved," 58.
3 context, "Ethno or Socio Poetics," 78.
4 above all the *cognitive model*, "No Humans Involved," 55.
5 discontinuous with evolution, "Re-enchantment of Humanism" (David Scott interview), 190.
6 induced to so perceive themselves, "No Humans Involved," 47.
7 the systematic nature of the rules which governed their exclusion, "No Humans Involved," 36.
8 code made flesh, "Human Being as Noun?," 78.
9 the misrecognition of human kinship, "No Humans Involved," 68.
10 no longer that of *only* being black, "No Humans Involved," 59.
11 every form of life that has ever been, "Re-enchantment of Humanism," 196.
12 alterable, "Rethinking 'Aesthetics,'" 271.

nunánuk

1 flesh, "Ceremony Must Be Found," 26.
2 economic, "Ethno or Socio Poetics," 81.
3 orthodoxy, "Ethno or Socio Poetics," 79.
4 *capital* with the rise of the global, "No Humans Involved," 63.
5 our different *generational* standpoints, "Re-enchantment of Humanism" (David Scott interview), 168.

Boda

1 then there is nothing I can't do, "Re-enchantment of Humanism" (David Scott interview), 148.
2 the well-being of the *human*, "No Humans Involved," 64.
3 exposes all the injustices inherent in structure, "No Humans Involved," 68.
4 mode of knowing, "Ethno or Socio Poetics," 82.
5 across the long wet hell of an ocean sea, "Re-enchantment of Humanism," 193.

Anguilla

1 human-in-itself, "No Humans Involved," 49.
2 context, "Ethno or Socio Poetics," 78.
3 context, "Ethno or Socio Poetics, " 78.
4 a WE that needed no OTHER, "Ethno or Socio Poetics," 85.
5 THE CATALYST FOR THAT TOTAL, "Ethno or Socio Poetics," 82.
6 other, "Ethno or Socio Poetics," 78.
7 alien, "Ethno or Socio Poetics," 81.
8 periphery, "Ethno or Socio Poetics," 82.
9 we, "Ethno or Socio Poetics," 78.
10 narrative of human emancipation, "No Humans Involved," 48.
11 races, "Ethno or Socio Poetics," 80.
12 created, "Ethno or Socio Poetics," 82.
13 every form of life that has ever been, "Re-enchantment of Humanism" (David Scott interview), 196.
14 nature, "Ethno or Socio Poetics," 81.
15 change in the relation to nature, "Ethno or Socio Poetics," 82.
16 conceal-oversee, "Ethno or Socio Poetics," 86.
17 what had lain, "On How We Mistook the Map for the Territory," 113.
18 THE RECLAMATION OF VAST AREAS OF OUR BEING, "Ethno or Socio Poetics," 82.

another set of instructions

1 ceremony-not-quite-found-then, "Human Being as Noun?," 6.
2 make, "Ethno or Socio Poetics," 78.
3 unblocking, "Human Being as Noun?," 75.
4 ultimately, "Rethinking 'Aesthetics,'" 253.

5 archeo-astronomers, "Re-enchantment of Humanism" (David Scott interview), 175.
6 is therefore a condition of each other's truth, "No Humans Involved," 67.

red august

1 flesh, "The Ceremony Must Be Found," 26.
2 *not* an accident, "Ethno or Socio Poetics," 79.
3 *such a taste* (from Augusta's grandmother), "Rethinking 'Aesthetics,'" 259.
4 ostensibly evolutionarily delivered genetic organizing principle, "No Humans Involved," 53.
5 relation, "Ethno or Socio Poetics," 78.
6 heresy, "Ethno or Socio Poetics," 79.
7 savages, "Ethno or Socio Poetics," 82.
8 a doubled pariah status, "No Humans Involved," 59.
9 could not be seen as costs, "No Humans Involved," 62.
10 disobedient by-nature, "Human Being as Noun?," 4.
11 global, "Ethno or Socio Poetics," 80.
12 expression, "Ethno or Socio Poetics," 79.
13 being human as praxis, "Human Being as Noun?," 9.
14 THE ONE, "Ethno or Socio Poetics," 82.
15 act of magic, "Ethno or Socio Poetics," 79.
16 more devalued, "Ethno or Socio Poetics," 81.
17 labour, "Ethno or Socio Poetics," 81.

relation

1 IN FACT IT IS HERE THAT I WOULD LIKE TO MAKE A CENTRAL POINT, "Ethno or Socio Poetics," 78.

prophet

1 stable replication of the invariant relation, "No Humans Involved," 58.
2 cheap labour far away, "Ethno or Socio Poetics," 80.
3 THE OTHER, "Ethno or Socio Poetics," 79.
4 self-making, "Ethno or Socio Poetics," 79.
5 rapidly accelerating post-industrial category, "No Humans Involved," 59.

6 freed itself from its dependence on *labor*, "No Humans Involved," 63.

7 knowledge must be rewritten, "No Humans Involved," 69.

8 therefore be more or less human, "No Humans Involved," 54.

9 by its highest degree of its nigger dysgenicity, "No Humans Involved," 51.

10 the goal of Material Redemption, "No Humans Involved," 61.

11 feels about, "Rethinking 'Aesthetics,'" 271.

12 of any other issue, "Human Being as Noun?," 3.

13 status quo, "Ethno or Socio Poetics," 79.

14 consciousness, "Ethno or Socio Poetics," 81.

15 temporary, "Ethno or Socio Poetics," 84.

and

1 he is, they are, the truth, "No Humans Involved," 70.

2 mean, "Rethinking 'Aesthetics,'" 266.

3 the center of the universe as its dregs, "Unsettling the Coloniality of Being/Power/Truth/Freedom," 278.

skin

1 otherness, "Ethno or Socio Poetics," 79.

2 operative, "Ethno or Socio Poetics," 78.

3 out of all proportions, "No Humans Involved," 47.

4 index, "Rethinking 'Aesthetics,'" 271.

5 an original handling of the Word (can give rise to) a new theoretical and heedless science *that poetry could already give an approximate notion of*, "Human Being as Noun?," 26.

losing it all

1 frontier, "Ethno or Socio Poetics," 79.

2 and you deny the abyss that lies about you, "Is 'Development' a Purely Empirical Concept or Also Teleological?," 299 (epigraph from Hanudon Kane).

3 do, "Rethinking 'Aesthetics,'" 266.

4 his modus operandi was to go around hitting all of us with a cane whether we had done anything or not. to wake up our minds he said! But he was an excellent teacher, "Re-enchantment of Humanism" (David Scott interview), 123.

5 even more totally so, "Unsettling the Coloniality of Being/Power/ Truth/Freedom," 303.

it's your father

1 with all my soul I wish for this opening, "Is 'Development' a Purely Empirical Concept or Also Teleological?" (epigraph), 299.
2 it is we who institute that truth, "No Humans Involved," 70.
3 wounds in the flesh, "Re-enchantment of Humanism" (David Scott interview), 151 (citing Fitzroy Frazier).
4 earlier episteme, "No Humans Involved," 62.
5 all middle-class subjects, "No Humans Involved," 61.
6 at the level of class, "No Humans Involved," 66.
7 absolutism of its related economic ethic, "No Humans Involved," 61.
8 human activities are responsible for global warming, "Human Being as Noun?," 1.
9 instrumental, "Ethno or Socio Poetics," 84.
10 nonmeasurable, noncomparable each to the other, "Ceremony Found," 307.
11 behavior-*prescriptive* status, "No Humans Involved," 62.
12 concrete, "Ethno or Socio Poetics," 79.
13 ostensibly evolutionarily retarded, "No Humans Involved," 52.
14 owe our *group presence*, "No Humans Involved," 36.
15 the moment, like a raft, carries you, "Is 'Development' a Purely Empirical Concept or Also Teleological?," 313.
16 central linkages . . . vital to tradition, and the crossings over in and between traditions, "Human Being as Noun?," 6, citing Bloom.
17 radically shortened, "On How We Mistook the Map for the Territory," 117.
18 natural, "Ceremony Must Be Found," 26.

edict

1 the *Bantustans* in which we have been trapped, "No Humans Involved," 56.
2 their conceptual others are those who make possible their accelerated enrichment, "No Humans Involved," 64.
3 *induced*, "Rethinking 'Aesthetics,'" 259.
4 the asylum catching fire, "Re-enchantment of Humanism" (David Scott interview), 124.

5　divinely condemned to be *fixed* and *motionless* at the center of the universe, "Human Being as Noun?," 12.
6　*as such an order,* "Rethinking 'Aesthetics,'" 255.

edgegrove

1　owe our *group presence,* "No Humans Involved," 36.
2　but also to propose, "Rethinking 'Aesthetics,'" 272.
3　normal, "Rethinking 'Aesthetics,'" 271.
4　the classical *episteme,* "No Humans Involved," 61.
5　generates conscious change in all subjects, "No Humans Involved," 68.
6　by those whom we ourselves have educated, "No Humans Involved," 43.
7　what was wrong with their education?, "No Humans Involved," 60.
8　what was wrong with their education?, "No Humans Involved," 60.

unlearning herself

1　the entropic falling apart, "Human Being as Noun?," 53.
2　in the wake of the cognitive mutation of humanism, "Is 'Development' a Purely Empirical Concept or Also Teleological?," 304.
3　pre-analytic premise, "Is 'Development' a Purely Empirical Concept or Also Teleological?," 308.
4　discardable throwaway status, "No Humans Involved," 63.
5　social mobility out of the gutters, "No Humans Involved," 64.
6　the divine truth of the scholastics, "Is 'Development' a Purely Empirical Concept or Also Teleological?," 306.
7　explosive psychic emancipation, "On How We Mistook the Map for the Territory," 13.
8　apologies to June Jordan, "On How We Mistook the Map for the Territory" (title).
9　the jobless category, "No Humans Involved," 42.
10　but as their extreme nigger form, "Unsettling the Coloniality of Being/Power/Truth/Freedom," 307.
11　fugitive truth, "Unsettling the Coloniality of Being/Power/Truth/Freedom" (citing Geertz), 282 .
12　*that which we have made,* we can unmake, then consciously remake, "Human Being as Noun?," 75.
13　redemptive prophetic, "Human Being as Noun?," 47 (citing Bogues).

birth chorus

1 the correlated otherness continuum, "Human Being as Noun?," 22.

2 les damnés, "No Humans Involved," 65.

3 we still have no name, "Re-enchantment of Humanism" (David Scott interview), 137.

4 the state of the planetary, "Is 'Development' a Purely Empirical Concept or Also Teleological?," 299.

5 unlike the working-class jobholders *cannot be seen*, "No Humans Involved," 64.

6 overrating our present global behaviors, "Is 'Development' a Purely Empirical Concept or Also Teleological?," 310.

7 life, "Ceremony Must Be Found," 26.

8 the enduring of the global ours, "Rethinking 'Aesthetics,'" 270.

9 the price paid for *our* well-being, "No Humans Involved," 70.

10 rigorously abductive, "Human Being as Noun?," 18.

11 must constrain, "Rethinking 'Aesthetics,'" 238.

12 to debaptize, "Is 'Development' a Purely Empirical Concept or Also Teleological?" (epigraph), 299.

13 took place *in the absence of* that new, "No Humans Involved," 68.

14 the well-being of the species: of universal individual human welfare, "Is 'Development' a Purely Empirical Concept or Also Teleological?," 312.

15 the collective ensemble of behaviors, "Is 'Development' a Purely Empirical Concept or Also Teleological?," 299.

16 justice, not as grim retribution, but as shared happiness, "Re-enchantment of Humanism" (David Scott interview), 124.

conditions

1 unjustly deprived, "No Humans Involved," 64.

2 invention of the endemically jobless, "On How We Mistook the Map for the Territory," 8.

3 a member of the beneficiary generation, "On How We Mistook the Map for the Territory," 10.

4 eco-systemic sense of right, "Is 'Development' a Purely Empirical Concept or Also Teleological?," 312.

Jamaica

1 NON-WEST, "Ethno or Socio Poetics," 81.
2 mobilize the sign of blackness, "On How We Mistook the Map for the Territory," 7 (citing Dubey).

blood chorus

1 *only*, "Rethinking 'Aesthetics,'" 258.
2 the question now touched upon of who we are, "Human Being as Noun?," 1.
3 name, "Ethno or Socio Poetics," 87.
4 *poor and jobless*, "Rethinking 'Aesthetics,'" 257.
5 *positively marked/menstrual blood*, "Rethinking 'Aesthetics,'" 252.
6 ontological sovereignty, "Re-enchantment of Humanism" (David Scott interview), 136.
7 at the level of race, "No Humans Involved," 66.
8 nature, "Rethinking 'Aesthetics,'" 272.
9 existential contradiction, "Human Being as Noun?," 16.
10 objective understanding/inner eyes, "No Humans Involved," 54.
11 the exiled captive priests, "Human Being as Noun?," 24.

shop

1 how our present middle-class *mode* of the subject, "No Humans Involved," 64.
2 ostensibly divinely ordained caste, "No Humans Involved," 53.
3 hegemonic economic categories, "No Humans Involved," 61.
4 my own radicalization . . . has never ceased, "Re-enchantment of Humanism" (David Scott interview), 153.

orchard

1 the escape hatch is always to be found in the category of the liminal, "No Humans Involved," 66.
2 hegemony of *political categories* was finally displaced, "No Humans Involved," 61.
3 legitimate and *just*, "No Humans Involved," 62.
4 "protection" for *agricultural* producers, "No Humans Involved," 62.

5 a whole new system of ideas, "On How We Mistook the Map for the Territory," 1.

6 does not have to inquire into the truth, "No Humans Involved," 70.

cycle

1 the earth was a star and the stars were earths, "Ceremony Must Be Found," 30.

2 revolution, "Ethno or Socio Poetics," 79.

3 Fallen Flesh, "Human Being as Noun?," 15.

saving the planet

1 truth, "Ethno or Socio Poetics," 79.

2 no less systemic revalorization, "On How We Mistook the Map for the Territory," 13.

3 circularly verify, "Is 'Development' a Purely Empirical Concept or Also Teleological?," 307.

4 my essay can be seen to have failed to find the ceremony, "Human Being as Noun?," 6.

5 it was as if you were suddenly in a different dimension, "Re-enchantment of Humanism" (David Scott interview), 125.

6 decidable, "Rethinking 'Aesthetics,'" 262.

staying

1 land, "Ethno or Socio Poetics," 81.

2 that circle of people, "No Humans Involved," 44.

3 a member of the beneficiary generation, "On How We Mistook the Map for the Territory," 10.

4 seen as *costs* within the terms, "No Humans Involved," 61.

5 pre-analytic premise, "Is 'Development' a Purely Empirical Concept or Also Teleological?," 308.

6 sacrificial costs, "No Humans Involved," 47 (citing Rene Giradi).

letting go

1 desupernaturalizing, "Re-enchantment of Humanism" (David Scott interview), 178.

2 reborn, that is *initiated*, "Human Being as Noun?," 1.

3 who of the we, "Human Being as Noun?," 9.
4 evolutionary, "Rethinking Aesthetics,'" 257.
5 ways, "Rethinking 'Aesthetics,'" 259.
6 the unbearable wrongness of being, "On How We Mistook the Map for the Territory" (title).

crate dig

Source Riddims from Sylvia Wynter

Primary texts by Sylvia Wynter that are cited herein

"The Ceremony Must Be Found: After Humanism." *boundary 2* 12, no.
3 / 13, no. 1 (1984): 19–70.

"Ethno or Socio Poetics." *Alcheringa/Ethnopoetics* 2 (1976): 78–94.

"Human Being as Noun? Or Being Human as Praxis? Towards the Auto-
poetic Turn/Overturn: A Manifesto." Unpublished essay.

"Is 'Development' a Purely Empirical Concept or Also Teleological? A
Perspective from We the Underdeveloped." In *Prospects for Recovery
and Sustainable Development in Africa*, edited by Aguibou Yansané,
299–316. Westport, CT: Greenwood Press, 1996.

"No Humans Involved: An Open Letter to My Colleagues." In *Institute
N.H.I.*, vol. 1, no. 1, 42–73. Stanford, CA, 1994.

"On How We Mistook the Map for the Territory and Reimprisoned
Ourselves in Our Unbearable Wrongness of Being, of *Désêtre*: Black
Studies toward the Human Project." In *Not Only the Masters Tools:
African American Studies in the Theory and Practice*, edited by
Lewis Gordon and Jane Anna Gordon, 107–69. New York: Paradigm
Press, 2006.

"ProudFlesh Inter/Views: Sylvia Wynter." *ProudFlesh: New Afrikan
Journal of Culture, Politics and Consciousness* 4 (2006): 1–35.

"The Re-enchantment of Humanism: An Interview with Sylvia Wynter."
Small Axe 8 (September 2000): 119–207.

"Rethinking 'Aesthetics': Notes towards a Deciphering Practice." In *Ex-Iles: Essays on Caribbean Cinema*, edited by Mbye Cham, 237–79. Trenton, NJ: Africa World Press, 1992.

"Unsettling the Coloniality of Being/Power/Truth/Freedom: Towards the Human, after Man, Its Overrepresentation—an Argument." *CR: The New Centennial Review* 3, no. 3 (2003): 257–337.

Relevant texts by Sylvia Wynter that are not directly cited

"Africa, the West and the Analogy of Culture: The Cinematic Text after Man." In *Symbolic Narratives/African Cinemas: Audience, Theory and Moving Image,* edited by June Givanni, 25–76. London: British Film Institute, 2000.

"After the New Class: James, *Les Damnés,* and the Autonomy of Human Cognition." Paper presented at the conference "C. L. R. James: His Intellectual Legacies," Wellesley, MA, April 19–21, 1991.

"Afterword: Beyond Miranda's Meanings: Un/silencing the 'Demonic Ground' of Caliban's 'Woman.'" In *Out of the Kumbla: Caribbean Women and Literature,* edited by Carole Boyce Davies and Elaine Savory Fido, 355–72. Trenton, NJ: Africa World Press, 1990.

Beyond Liberal and Marxist Leninist Feminisms: Towards an Autonomous Frame of Reference. San Francisco: Institute for Research on Women and Gender, 1982.

"Beyond the Categories of the Master Conception: The Counter-doctrine of the Jamesian Poiesis." In *C. L. R. James's Caribbean,* edited by Paget Henry and Paule Buhle, 63–91. Durham: Duke University Press, 1992.

"Beyond the World of Man: Glissant and the New Discourse of the Antilles." *World Literature Today* 63 (Autumn 1989): 637–47.

"The Ceremony Found: Black Knowledges/Struggles, the Color Line and the Third Emancipatory Breaching of the Law of Cognitive Closure." Keynote paper presented at the Collegium for African American Research: Black Knowledges, Black Struggles, Civil Rights—Transnational Perspectives, University of Bremen, Germany, March 26, 2009.

"Columbus, the Ocean Blue and 'Fables That Stir the Mind': To Reinvent the Study of Letters." In *Poetics of the Americas: Race, Founding and Textuality,* edited by Bainard Cohen and Jefferson Humphries, 141–64. Baton Rouge: Louisiana State University Press, 1992.

"Conversation [with Daryl Cumber Dance]." In *New World Adams:*

Conversations with Contemporary West Indian Writers, edited by Daryl Cumber Dance, 276–82. Leeds, UK: Peepal Tree Press, 1992.

"Creole Criticism: A Critique." *New World Quarterly* 4 (1973): 12–36.

"A Different Kind of Creature: Caribbean Literature, the Cyclops Factor and the Second Poetics of the Propter Nos." *Annals of Scholarship* 12, nos. 1/2 (1997): 153–72.

Do Not Call Us Negroes: How Multicultural Textbooks Perpetuate Racism. San Jose, CA: Aspire Books, 1992.

"1492: A New World View." In *Race, Discourse, and the Origin of the Americas: A New World View*, edited by Vera Lawrence Hyatt and Rex Nettleford, 5–57. Washington, DC: Smithsonian Institution Press, 1995.

"Gender or the Genre of the Human? History, the Hard Task of Dessa Rose, and *the* Issue for the New Millennium." Paper presented at the symposium "Black Women Writers and the 'High Art' of Afro-American Letters," University of California, San Diego, May 15–17, 1998.

"'Genital Mutilation' or 'Symbolic Birth'? Female Circumcision, Lost Origins and the Aculturalism of Feminist/Western Thought." *Case Western Law Review, Colloquium: Bridging Society, Culture and Law: The Issue of Female Circumcision* 47, no. 2 (1997): 501–52.

The Hills of Hebron: A Jamaican Novel. New York: Simon and Schuster, 1962.

"Human Being as Noun, or Being Human as Praxis? On the Laws/Modes of Auto-Institution and Our Ultimate Crisis of Global Warming and Climate Change." Paper presented at the Distinguished Lecture and Residency Series at the Center for African American Studies, Wesleyan University, Middletown, CT, April 23, 2008.

"Jonkonnu in Jamaica: Towards the Interpretation of Folk Dance as a Cultural Process." *Jamaica Journal* 4, no. 2 (1970): 34–48.

Maskarade. In *West Indian Plays for Schools*, by Easton Lee, Sylvia Wynter, and Enid Chevannes, vol. 2, 26–55. Kingston, Jamaica: Jamaica Publishing House, 1979.

"Meditations on History: *Dessa Rose* and Slavery Revisited." Paper presented at the symposium "Black Women Writers and the 'High Art' of Afro-American Letters," University of California, San Diego, May 15–17, 1998.

"New Seville and the Conversion Experience of Bartolomé de Las Casas: Part One." *Jamaica Journal* 17, no. 2 (1984): 25–32.

"New Seville and the Conversion Experience of Bartolomé de Las Casas: Part Two." *Jamaica Journal* 17, no. 3 (1984): 46–55.

"Novel and History, Plot and Plantation." *Savacou* 5 (1971): 95–102.

"On Disenchanting Discourse: 'Minority' Literary Criticism and Beyond." *Cultural Critique* 7 (Fall 1987): 207–44.

"One Love: Rhetoric or Reality? Aspects of Afro-Jamaicanism." *Caribbean Studies* 12, no. 3 (1972): 64–97.

"The Pope Must Have Been Drunk, the King of Castile a Madman: Culture as Actuality and the Caribbean Rethinking of Modernity." In *Reordering of Culture: Latin America, the Caribbean and Canada in the 'Hood,* edited by Alvina Ruprecht and Cecilia Taiana, 17–41. Ottawa: Carleton University Press, 1995.

"Towards the Sociogenic Principle: Fanon, Identity and the Puzzle of Conscious Experience." In *National Identities and Socio-Political Changes in Latin America,* edited by Mercedes F. Durán-Cogan and Antonio Gómez-Moriana, 30–66. New York: Routledge, 2001.

"We Must Learn to Sit Down Together and Talk about a Little Culture: Reflections on West Indian Writing and Criticism." *Jamaica Journal* 2, no. 4 (1968): 27–42.

"We Must Learn to Sit Down Together and Talk about a Little Culture: Reflections on West Indian Writing and Criticism." *Jamaica Journal* 3, no. 1 (1969): 27–42.

"Yours in the Intellectual Struggle." In *The Caribbean Woman Writer as Scholar: Creating, Imagining, Theorizing,* edited by Keshia N. Abraham, 21–70. Coconut Creek, FL: Caribbean Studies Press, 2009.